COPYCAT RECIPES:

Learn the secrets of 200 delicious recipes.
A quick and easy to follow step-by-step
guide to make the most popular
restaurant dishes at home.

CHAYLA HENCK

Table Of Contents

Introduction

Our lifestyle and eating habits are doing something amazing. That means we eat without a daily schedule in a variety of places, without paying enough attention to what we consume. People's choices on whether to eat at home or in public dining are typically different. It is not shocking, because everyone has their own pace and preference for life.

Homemade cooking is more economical. Separately the quality of the items is much lower than that of the finished dish elsewhere in the cafeteria.

You know the composition all along. Most food manufacturers use toxic additives to improve the product's flavor or to increase its shelf-life. Also, we don't know the quality of the ingredients we used to cook the platter. We still know which ingredients we need to cook at home.

Homemade food may have calories and composition unbalanced. Unless the family passed the custom of unhealthy or excessively spicy food from generation to generation, then the homemade food will be a minus rather than a plus. By the way, there is even an aging theory. It says fatty and sweet foods make a contribution to the body's faster aging.

It takes time to prepare. This can be called a plus and a minus. Anyone who likes to cook will have free time to spend in the kitchen.

The dishes. Home cooked meals are indeed good because, besides you, you always know who is using your plates ad forks spoons—big advantage.

It is typically much easier to consume fresh food than dining at a restaurant or purchasing processed food from the store.

Why prefer homemade food over food from the restaurant?

On the off chance that we eat at a café, we're paying for the food as well as the expenses of running the store. The lights, the house, and the laborers — we eat other than the feast. The equivalent goes for supermarkets for pre-made or solidified suppers. Here are a few additional ways by following which you can set aside cash:

- Arranging numerous dinner days. On the off chance that we have an arrangement, or something previously made, we will be more averse to be enticed to eat something different

- Make a rundown of groceries and stick to it to abstain from purchasing extra food.

- Store any left in the ice chest or cooler. After you have put away load of extras, you can warm them thereafter when you lack the capacity to deal with cooking. This may seem like trying to grab something to eat at the local supermarket or driving at the nearest restaurant to get a take-out may be a quick and easy solution when you're in a rush. In reality, cooking something at home can be many times faster, particularly when you plan accordingly. So many meals can be made in under 30 minutes. And if you're choosing a more complicated recipe, you could always cook in bulk and eat or freeze the excess later that week.

Several foods that are commercially prepared are high in fat, salt, and sugar. So if we start preparing our food, we know precisely which ingredients are going into our food and how much of each is going into it. We are in control when we cook at home.

Home food arrangement can be especially advantageous in the event that you or a relative has a hypersensitivity to the food. You will diminish the danger of a hypersensitive response since you are accountable for your kitchen.

Several restaurants and quick-food joints offer much larger portions than is needed. And the thing is, if food is in front of you, you'll be eating it. You can limit the quantity of food served for the dinner when you dine in, reducing excessive temptation.

Eating at home gives time to the entire family to discuss their day. Studies show that our youngsters and families are a lot more joyful when we eat together. Eating together is related with stoutness, kids improving at school, and less substance abuse inside the family. It's a pleasant activity as well as an ideal thing to instruct them on great dietary patterns by including your children in food planning (possibly by requesting that they read the formula for all to hear or consolidate fixings).

Day after day, as you spend a short time each day making various kinds of foods for yourself or your mates, your cooking skills can gradually develop. It says practice makes a perfect person. For least you can prepare basic dishes because you're new to the kitchen and then, day by day, you can prepare more complicated meals slowly.

The food products that you made at home can keep your lifestyle healthy and you're eating habits good. If you can't control eating the food outside, then your life will be in distress.

Chapter 1:
Emotional Benefits and
Advantages of Cooking at Home

We all like the right food, but one of the easiest ways to improve our health is to prepare more home-cooked meals. This is the entry method.

Benefits of Home Cooking

Whether you are living alone or busy parents, finding time and energy to prepare home-cooked meals seems to be a difficult task. At the end of a busy day, eating out or ordering food seems to be the fastest and easiest option. But comfort food can negatively affect your mood and health.

Processed foods are usually rich in chemical additives, hormones, sugar, salt, unhealthy fats and calories, all of which can negatively affect your brain and your expectations. It can make you feel tired, swollen, irritable, depressed, stressed, anxious and other mental health problems. It will also affect your waistline. An ongoing report demonstrated that individuals who eat food consume an average of 200 calories per day than those who cook at home.

By cooking by yourself, you can ensure that you and your family eat fresh, healthy meals. This can help you look healthier, increase energy, stabilize weight and mood, and improve sleep and resist stress. When preparing food, you also know clearly what food you put into your body and how different foods affect your way of thinking and feeling.

Home cooking need not be too complicated. The cornerstone of a healthy diet is that the food you eat should be as natural as possible. This means that whenever possible, replace processed foods with real foods, and eat a lot of vegetables and healthy sources of protein. This doesn't imply that you ought to spend hours in the kitchen, joining many various fixings or following point by point plans. In fact, simple meals are usually the most delicious. And you don't have to take home every meal perfectly. Cooking at your own each week can be satisfying.

Home cooking is also a great way to get along with others-and you don't have to be a good chef. Regardless of your ability or experience as a chef, you can learn to prepare fast and healthy meals that have real benefits for your physical and mental health.

Health Benefits

Getting ready sound dinners at home can bolster your resistant framework and decrease the danger of sicknesses, for example, coronary illness, disease, hypertension and diabetes.

It can provide you with more energy, improve sleep at night, and help you better manage health problems.

In women, healthy food cooking can help reduce menstrual symptoms, menopause and increase fertility.

On the off chance that you are on an exceptional eating routine or attempting to shed pounds, at that point getting ready suppers for yourself will permit you to more readily control the fixings and the measure of dinners you eat, thereby better controlling your weight or dealing with food allergies.

By handling food safely while cooking at home, you are less likely to suffer from foodborne illness.

Home cooking can make your brain smarter, fight cognitive decline and reduce the risk of Alzheimer's disease.

It can stabilize children's energy and help them grow into healthy, confident adults.

Enjoy Sharing Home Cooked Meals

Food brings people together, and home cooking is a great way to reunite with family at the table. Everyone loves home cooking, even grumpy or fussy teenagers. In the event that you live alone, this doesn't imply that you need to cook or eat alone. Offering suppers to others is an incredible method to extend informal organizations. Getting random comments about a meal you prepared for someone can also improve your self-esteem.

Make mealtime a social experience. The simple act of chatting with friends or relatives at the table can play an important role in relieving stress and improving mood. Bring your family together and keep each other up to date. If you live alone, please invite friends, colleagues or neighbors.

Turn off the screen. Take a break from the TV, and maintain a strategic distance from other interference until you have a real chance to communicate with the person you are dining with. By avoiding screens and eating with others, this will also help avoid overeating.

Cook with others. Invite your husband, roommate or friend to share shopping and cooking duties-for example, one prepares participants and the other is dessert. Cooking with others may be a fun way to deepen interpersonal relationships and share expenses, which may make both of you cheaper.

Overcoming the Obstacles of Home Cooking

Despite the many benefits, many of us still consider preparing meals as housework, either because we don't have time to do it, or only for professional chefs. Maybe you have tried cooking before and don't like the end result, or your child prefers to eat out?

Overcoming obstacles to home cooking usually starts with changing the way you prepare meals or the time you spend in the kitchen. Some common reasons for not cooking at home and our treatment methods include:

Difficulty 1: "No time to cook."

Of course, it may take a long time after shopping, cutting ingredients, cooking and cleaning. But there are many ways to speed it up:

Online shopping, all ingredients are at your doorstep.

Share with friends and family. Replace the shopping and cleaning work of your husband or your neighbor.

Instead of watching a cooking show on the sofa, it is better to move the TV to the kitchen and follow it.

Multitasking: chat or watch TV on the phone while cooking.

Purchase pre-washed thinly sliced vegetable bags and place all food in a steamer or pot for a healthy meal in a short time.

When the ingredients and recipes come to your door, please try the door-to-door service.

Make some preparations in advance. For example, chopping vegetables while reducing stress on weekends to reduce the final cooking time.

Use fresh ingredients. Raw food recipes can be prepared in just a few minutes.

Show the meal as a pleasant and relaxing experience, not as trivial-it looks like it will take almost no time.

2: "It's cheap to eat fast food."

At first glance, eating at a fast food restaurant seems cheaper than preparing home-cooked meals. But this rarely happens. A study by the University Of Washington School Of Public Health showed that people who cook at home tend to follow healthier eating habits without increasing food costs.

3: Am tired to cook

Creating a healthy diet should not cost a lot of energy.

Loading meat and vegetables in a slow cooker in the morning will allow you to go home and cook at night, with little preparation required and almost no cleaning.

At the point when you don't have the opportunity or vitality to cook, set up an enormous supper and afterward freeze the rest of the extras into little bits.

By cooking significant proteins once per week (such as roast chicken or slow-cooked turkey breasts), you can use meat to prepare quick and easy meals such as soups, salads, sandwiches, burritos or pasta within a week.

4: "I can't cook"

Within the occasion that you simply are focused over the chance of setting up your own dinners, make certain to recall that cooking isn't an accurate science.

It is usually very good to skip one component or replace it with another.

Search or buy basic recipes online for simple recipe tips.

Like anything else, the more cooking, the better. Even if you are a complete beginner in the kitchen, you will soon master some healthy and fast meals.

5: "I hate being in the kitchen."

If you despise investing energy in the kitchen, you have to grasp your fascinating side. Cooking doesn't work, this is diversion!

Play your favorite music, pour a glass of wine, and then dance while chopping and peeling.

Or listen to audio books and get lost in a good story.

Chapter 2:
Breakfast Recipe

1. IHOP's Buttermilk Pancake

Preparation time: 5 minutes

Cooking time: 8 minutes

Servings: 8 to 10

INGREDIENTS

1¼ cups all-purpose flour

1 teaspoon baking soda

1 teaspoon baking powder

1¼ cups granulated sugar

1 pinch salt

1 egg

1¼ cups buttermilk

¼ cup cooking oil

DIRECTIONS

Preheat your pan by leaving it over medium heat while you are preparing the pancake batter.

Take all of your dry ingredients and mix them together.

Take all of your wet ingredients and mix them together.

Carefully combine the dry mixture into the wet mixture until everything is mixed together completely.

Melt some butter in your pan.

Slowly pour batter into the pan until you have a 5-inch circle.

Flip the pancake when its edges seem to have hardened.

Cook the other side of the hotcake as well.

Repeat steps six through eight until your batter is finished.

`Serve with softened butter and maple syrup.

NUTRITION: Calories 180.1 Total Fat 7.9 G Carbohydrates 23.2 G Protein 4.1 G, Sodium 271.6 Mg

2. Starbucks's Marble Pound Cake

Preparation Time: 10 minutes

Cooking Time: 1 hour 30 minutes

Servings: 16

INGREDIENTS

4½ cups cake flour

2 teaspoons baking powder

⅛ Teaspoon salt

6 ounces semisweet chocolate, finely chopped

2 cups unsalted butter, softened

3 cups granulated sugar

1 tablespoon vanilla

1 lemon, grated for zest

10 large eggs

2 tablespoons orange liquor OR milk

DIRECTIONS

Assemble your ingredients, and then:

Preheat the oven to 350°F;

Grease a 10×4-inch tube pan;

Line the pan's bottom with greased wax paper; and

Flour the entire pan.

Sift together the cake flour, baking powder, and salt in a medium-sized bowl—this is your dry mixture.

Melt the chocolate in a medium-sized bowl, then beat in the butter. When the mixture is smooth, beat in the sugar, lemon zest, and vanilla until the liquid mixture is uniform.

When the mixture is fully beaten, beat in the eggs, two at a time, until the mixture looks curdled.

Pour half of your dry mixture into your liquid mixture and mix until blended.

Add the orange liquor and the rest of the dry mixture. Continue beating the mixture.

When the mixture is blended, use a spatula to start folding it—this is your batter.

Set aside 4 cups of the batter. Whisk the softened chocolate with the batter.

Now that you have a light batter and a dark batter, place the batter into the tube pan by the spoonful, alternating between the two colors.

When the pan is full, shake it slightly to level the batter. Run a knife through the batter to marble it.

Put the dish within the stove and heat for an hour and 15 minutes. In case there are still a few damp pieces on the toothpick after you take it out, at that point the cake is done.

Remove the cake and leave it to rest overnight.

NUTRITION: Calories 582.1 Total Fat 32 G Carbohydrates 69.6 G Protein 8.6 G Sodium 114.8 Mg

3. IHOP's Scrambled Egg

Preparation Time: 5 minutes

Cooking Time: 5 minutes

Servings: 1

INGREDIENTS

¼ cup pancake mix

1–2 tablespoons butter

6 large eggs

Salt and pepper, to taste

DIRECTIONS

Thoroughly beat the pancake mix and the eggs together until no lumps or clumps remain.

Butter a pan over medium heat.

When the pan is hot enough, pour the egg mixture in the middle of the pan.

Add the salt and pepper and let the mixture sit for about a minute.

When the egg starts cooking, start pushing the edges of the mixture toward the middle of the pan. Continue until the entire mixture is cooked.

Serve and enjoy.

NUTRITION: Calories 870 Total Fat 54 G Carbohydrates 9 G Protein 69 G Sodium 34.9 Mg

4. Starbucks's Chocolate Cinnamon Bread

Preparation Time: 15 minutes

Cooking Time: 1 hour

Servings: 16

INGREDIENTS

Bread:

1½ cups unsalted butter

3 cups granulated sugar

5 large eggs

2 cups flour

1¼ cups processed cocoa

1 tablespoon ground cinnamon

1 teaspoon salt

½ teaspoon baking powder

½ teaspoon baking soda

¼ cup water

1 cup buttermilk

1 teaspoon vanilla extract

Topping:

¼ cup granulated sugar

½ teaspoon cinnamon

½ teaspoon processed cocoa

⅛ Teaspoon ginger, ground

⅛ Teaspoon cloves, ground

DIRECTIONS

Before cooking:

Preheat the oven to 350°F;

Grease two 9×5×3 loaf pans; and

Line the bottoms of the pans with wax paper.

Cream the sugar by beating it with the butter.

Beat the eggs into the mixture one at a time.

Sift the flour, cocoa, cinnamon, salt, baking powder, and baking soda into a large bowl.

In another bowl, whisk together the water, buttermilk, and vanilla.

Make a well in the dry mixture and start pouring in the wet mixtures a little at a time, while whisking.

When the mixture starts becoming doughy, divide it in two and transfer it to the pans.

Mix together all the topping ingredients and sprinkle evenly on top of the mixture in both pans.

Bake for 50 to 60 minutes, or until the bread has set.

NUTRITION: Calories 370 Total Fat 14 G Carbohydrates 59 G Protein 7 G Sodium 270 Mg

5. Waffle House's Waffle

Preparation Time: 5 minutes

Cooking Time: 20 minutes

Servings: 6

INGREDIENTS

1½ cups all-purpose flour

1 teaspoon salt

½ teaspoon baking soda

1 egg

½ cup + 1 tablespoon granulated white sugar

2 tablespoons butter, softened

2 tablespoons shortening

½ cup half-and-half

½ cup milk

¼ cup buttermilk

¼ teaspoon vanilla

DIRECTIONS

Prepare the dry mixture by sifting the flour into a bowl and mixing it with the salt and baking soda.

In a medium bowl, lightly beat an egg. When the egg has become frothy, beat in the butter, sugar, and shortening. When the mixture is thoroughly mixed, beat in the half-and-half, vanilla, milk, and buttermilk. Continue beating the mixture until it is smooth.

While beating the wet mixture, slowly pour in the dry mixture, making sure to mix thoroughly and remove all the lumps.

Chill the batter overnight (optional but recommended; if you can't chill the mixture overnight, leave it for at least 15 to 20 minutes).

Take the batter out of the refrigerator. Preheat and grease your waffle iron.

Cook each waffle for three to four minutes. Serve with butter and syrup.

NUTRITION: Calories 313.8 Total Fat 12.4 G Carbohydrates 45 G Protein 5.9 G Sodium 567.9 Mg

6. Mimi's Café Santa Fé Omelet

Preparation Time: 10 minutes

Cooking Time: 10 minutes

Servings: 1

INGREDIENTS

Chipotle Sauce:

    1 cup marinara or tomato sauce

    ¾ cup water

    ½ cup chipotle in adobo sauce

    1 teaspoon kosher salt

Omelet:

1 tablespoon onions, diced

1 tablespoon jalapeños, diced

2 tablespoons cilantro, chopped

2 tablespoons tomatoes, diced

¼ cup fried corn tortillas, cut into strips

3 eggs, beaten

2 slices cheese

1 dash of salt and pepper

Garnish:

2 ounces chipotle sauce, hot

¼ cup fried corn tortillas, cut into strips

1 tablespoon sliced green onions

1 tablespoon guacamole

DIRECTIONS

Melt some butter in a pan over medium heat, making sure to coat the entire pan.

Sauté the jalapeños, cilantro, tomatoes, onions, and tortilla strips for about a minute.

Add the eggs, seasoning them with salt and pepper and stirring occasionally. Flip the omelet when it has set. Place the cheese on the top half.

When the cheese starts to become melty, fold the omelet in half and transfer to a plate.

Garnish the omelet with chipotle sauce, guacamole, green onions, and corn tortillas.

NUTRITION: Calories 519 Total Fat 32 G Carbohydrates 60 G Protein 14 G Sodium 463 Mg

7. Alice Springs Chicken from Outback

Preparation Time: 5 minutes

Cooking Time: 2 hours 30 minutes

Servings: 4

INGREDIENTS

Sauce:

½ cup Dijon mustard - ½ cup honey

¼ cup mayonnaise - 1 teaspoon fresh lemon juice

Chicken preparation:

4 chicken breast, boneless and skinless

2 tablespoons butter - 1 tablespoon olive oil

8 ounces fresh mushrooms, sliced

4 slices bacon, cooked and cut into 2-inch pieces

2 ½ cups Monterrey Jack cheese, shredded

Parsley for serving (optional)

DIRECTIONS

Preheat oven to 400 °F.

Mix together ingredients for the sauce in a bowl.

Put chicken in a Ziploc bag, then add sauce into bag until only ¼ cup is left. Keep remaining sauce in a container, cover, and refrigerate. Make sure to seal Ziploc bag tightly and shake gently until chicken is coated with sauce Keep in refrigerator for at least 2 hours.

Melt butter in a pan over medium heat. Toss in mushrooms and cook for 5 minutes or until brown. Remove from pan and place on a plate.

In an oven-safe pan, heat oil. Place marinated chicken flat in pan and cook for 5 minutes on each side or until both sides turn golden brown.

Top with even amounts of mushroom, bacon, and cheese. Cover pan with oven-safe lid, then bake for 10 to 15 minutes until chicken is cooked through. Remove lid and bake an additional 1-3 minutes until the cheese is all melted.

Transfer onto a plate. Serve with remaining sauce on the side. Sprinkle chicken with parsley if desired

NUTRITION: Calories 888Total Fat 56 G Carbohydrates 41 G Protein 59 G Sodium 1043 Mg

8. Oriental Salad from Applebee's

Preparation Time: 15 minutes

Cooking Time: 5 minutes

Servings: 6

INGREDIENTS

3 tablespoons honey

1½ tablespoons rice wine vinegar

¼ cup mayonnaise

1 teaspoon Dijon mustard

⅛ teaspoon sesame oil

3 cups vegetable oil, for frying

2 chicken breasts, cut into thin strips

1 egg

1 cup milk

1 cup flour

1 cup breadcrumbs

1 teaspoon salt

¼ teaspoon pepper

3 cups romaine lettuce, diced

½ cup red cabbage, diced

½ cup napa cabbage, diced

1 carrot, grated

¼ cup cucumber, diced

3 tablespoons sliced almonds

¼ cup dry chow mein

DIRECTIONS

To make the dressing, add honey, rice wine vinegar, mayonnaise, Dijon mustard, and sesame oil to a blender. Mix until well combined. Store in refrigerator until ready to serve.

Heat oil in a deep pan over medium-high heat.

As oil warms, whisk together egg and milk in a bowl. In another bowl, add flour, breadcrumbs, salt, and pepper. Mix well.

Dredge chicken strips in egg mixture, then in the flour mixture. Make sure the chicken is coated evenly on all sides. Shake off any excess.

Deep fry chicken strips for about 3 to 4 minutes until thoroughly cooked and lightly brown. Transfer onto a plate lined with paper towels to drain and cool. Work in batches, if necessary.

Chop strips into small, bite-size pieces once cool enough to handle.

Next, prepare salad by adding romaine, red cabbage, napa cabbage, carrots, and cucumber to a serving bowl. Top with chicken pieces, almonds, and chow mein. Drizzle prepared dressing on top.

Serve immediately.

NUTRITION: Calories 384Total Fat 13 G Saturated Fat 3 G Carbohydrates 40 G Sugar 13 G Fibers 2 G Protein 27 G Sodium 568 Mg

9. Bacon Muffins

Preparation time: 5 min

Cooking time: 15 minutes

Servings: 4

Ingredients:

12.7oz flour

Salt Pepper

Egg

1 tsp parsley

Four bacon pieces

7.8fl oz milk

Onion

2 tbsp. olive oil

3.5ounce Cheddar cheese

2 tsp powder

Directions:

Preheat oven to 190C/170C fan forced. Line a 12-hole, 1/3 cup–capacity muffin pan with paper cases.

Heat oil in a medium frying pan over medium-high heat. Add bacon. Cook for 5 minutes or until crisp. Cool.

Combine sifted flour with pepper, cheese, chives and bacon in a medium bowl. Make a well in the center. Add remaining ingredients, stirring until combined.

Spoon mixture into paper cases. Bake for 20-25 minutes or until golden and just firm to touch. Stand in pan for 5 minutes. Transfer to wire rack to cool.

Nutrition: Calories: 350 Fat: 18g Carbohydrates: 32g Protein: 16gram

10.   Breakfast Muffins

Preparation time: 20 minutes

Cooking time: 20 minutes

Servings: 2

Ingredients:

New Thyme 1.49fl oz almond milk

Handfuls lettuce cooked veggies

Salt Pepper

1 tbsp. coriander

3oz granola

Directions:

Preheat the oven to 375 degrees. Coat 6 cups of a muffin tin with cooking spray or line with paper liners.

Crack the eggs into a large bowl. Use a Braun MultiQuick

Hand Blender or a whisk to blend the eggs until smooth, this will take less than a minute.

Add the spinach, bacon and cheese to the egg mixture and stir to combine.

Divide the egg mixture evenly among the muffin cups.

Bake for 15-18 minutes or until eggs are set.

Serve immediately or store in the refrigerator until ready to eat. Top with diced tomatoes and parsley if desired.

Nutrition: 440 Fat: 28g Carbohydrates: 28gProtein:19grams

11.   Buttermilk Biscuits

Preparation time: 15 minutes

Cooking time: 25 minutes

Servings: 3

Ingredients:

2 cups bread Salt

1 tsp sugar

1/2 tsp powder

3/4 cup buttermilk

Honey Butter

4 tbsp butter

1/4 tsp soda

Directions:

 Make sure your baking powder and baking soda are still fresh before starting. Both ingredients are important to get a good rise in these biscuits.

Be sure to use cold butter and buttermilk in these biscuits. Prepare your dry ingredients first, then take your butter and buttermilk out of the refrigerator to ensure that they are cold.

Don't overwork your dough, make sure to work it together very gently.

Be sure to fold the dough into thirds and pat it down three times. This helps to ensure that your biscuits are super flaky.

When cutting your biscuits out, don't twist your cutter. This will seal off the edges of your dough and they won't rise as high. Just cut the dough straight down and pull the cutter right back out. I like to flour the biscuit cutter to make sure the biscuit dough doesn't stick too.

Lay the biscuits on a baking sheet touching each other. This will help them rise taller and give them soft edges when you pull them apart!

Nutrition: calories 103 Fat: 5g Carbohydrates: 14g Protein:17g

12.   Cheese on Soft Toast

Preparation time: 10 minutes

Cooking time: 15 minutes

Servings: 4

Ingredients:

6.2ounce milk - 1 tsp yeast - two tbsp condensed milk

8.8ounce bread - 1.4ounce butter

0.42ounce milk powder

Salt Sugar Herbs

1/2 cup cheddar cheese

Directions:

Preheat oven to 250C (480F). Generously butter bread and place on a baking tray lined with foil or baking paper.Bake for 3 minutes or until butter is melted.

Top with slices of cheese to completely cover the bread. Bake for another 5 minutes or until the cheese is melted and bubbling with golden brown patches.

Nutrition: Calories: 60 Fat: 1g Carbohydrates s: 7g Protein: 12g

13.   Cookies with dark chocolate

Preparation time: 10 minutes

Cooking time: 10 minutes

Servings: 8

Ingredients:

10.6ounce bread Salt

4.4ounce butter

4.4ounce black chocolate

5.3ounce sugar

2 tsp vanilla essence

2 eggs

1 tbsp honey

Directions:

HEAT oven to 325° F. baking sheets with parchment paper or lightly grease.

Soften 2/3 cup morsels in bowl on MEDIUM-HIGH control the power for 30 seconds; Blend. Pieces may hold a few of their unique shape. Microwave at extra

10- to 15-second interims, blending fair until pieces are dissolved. Set aside.

Filter flour, cocoa, preparing pop and salt into bowl. Mix butter, brown sugar and granulated sugar in expansive blender bowl until velvety. Include dissolved chocolate and blend well. Include egg and vanilla extricate, blending until well mixed, around 1 miniature. Include flour blend, blending fair until mixed. Mix in remaining 1 glass pieces. Drop mixture by level 1/4-cup degree 3 inches separated onto arranged preparing sheets.

Prepare for 16 to 18 minutes or until wooden choose embedded in center comes out with damp scraps and the tops have a split appearance. Cool on preparing sheets for 5 minutes. Evacuate to wire rack to cool totally.

Nutrition: Calories: 83 Fat: 2gCarbohydrates: 15g Protein: 3grams

14.   Corn Pudding with Bacon

Preparation time: 10 minutes

Cooking time: 60 minutes

Servings: 7

Ingredients:

4 tablespoons bacon

2 tsp garlic

1 tbsp butter

1 1/2 cup milk Onion

1/2 Bell-pepper

Thyme leaves

1/2 cup lotions

2 tsp corn

1/4 cup lettuce

3 cups cubed bread

3 tbsp Parmesan Salt Pepper

1 cup pasta

Directions:

Preheat oven to 325 degrees F.

Grease a 2-quart baking dish with margarine.

Cook 3 slices of bacon until crispy.

Cut bacon into small pieces.

Melt butter.

Mix eggs, butter and spices together in a bowl.

Then add flour, creamed corn, light cream, & bacon and mix together until flour lumps are smooth.

Pour mixture into the baking dish.

Bake for 90 minutes

As it cools, the corn pudding deflates.

Serve warm. Enjoy!

Nutrition: Calories: 360 Fat: 21g Carbohydrates: 60g Protein: 23grams

15.   Egg Rolls

Preparation time: 5 min

Cooking time: 7 min

Servings: 6

Ingredients:

0.35-pound beef

3/4 cup cabbage egg roll wrappers

Spray to prevent sticking

Directions:

Warm the 2 teaspoons of vegetable oil in a huge dish over medium tall warm. Include the ground pork and season it with salt and pepper. Cook the pork with a spatula, until meat is browned and cooked through. Include the garlic and ginger at that point

Mix within the coleslaw blend and green onions. Cook until cabbage is shriveled. Stir the soy sauce and sesame oil, at that point evacuate from heat. Spoon roughly 2-3 tablespoons of filling onto each egg roll wrapper and crease concurring to bundle headings.

Pour 2-3 inches of oil into a profound pot. Heat the oil to 350 degrees. Broil 3-4 egg rolls at a time, turning sometimes, until browned all over, roughly 3-5 minutes. Drain on paper towels, at that point serve with plunging sauce of your choice.

Nutrition: Calories: 140 Fat: 16g Carbohydrates: 2g Protein: 2grams

16. The French Toasts from Denny's

Preparation Time: 10 minutes

Cooking Time: 12 minutes

Servings: 6

Ingredients

Batter:

4 eggs

⅔ Cup whole milk

⅓ Cup flour

⅓ Cup sugar

½ teaspoon vanilla extract

¼ teaspoon salt

⅛ Teaspoon cinnamon

6 slices bread loaf, sliced thick

3 tablespoons butter

Powdered sugar for dusting

Syrup as desired

Directions

Mix in the ingredients for batter in a bowl.

Soak bread slices in batter one at a time for at least 30 seconds on both sides. Allow excess batter to drip off. Soften 1 tablespoon of butter in a skillet, cook battered bread over medium warm for 2 minutes or until each side is brilliant brown. Move slice to a plate.

Repeat with the remaining slices of bread, adding more butter to the pan if needed.

Dust with powdered sugar, if desired, and with syrup poured on top.

Nutrition: Calories 264, Total Fat 11 g, Carbohydrates 33 g, Protein 8 g, Sodium 360 mg

17. McDonald's Sausage Egg McMuffin

Preparation Time: 10 minutes

Cooking Time: 15 minutes

Servings: 4

Ingredients

4 English muffins, cut in half horizontally

4 slices American processed cheese

½ tablespoon oil - 1-pound ground pork, minced

½ teaspoon dried sage, ground

½ teaspoon dried thyme - 1 teaspoon onion powder

¾ teaspoon black pepper - ¾ teaspoon salt

½ teaspoon white sugar

4 large ⅓-inch onion ring slices

4 large eggs

2 tablespoons water

Directions

Preheat oven to 300°F.

Cover one half of muffin with cheese, leaving one half uncovered. Transfer both halves to a baking tray. Place in oven.

For the sausage patties, use your hands to mix pork, sage, thyme, onion powder, pepper, salt, and sugar in a bowl. Form into 4 patties. Make sure they are slightly larger than the muffins.

Heat oil in a pan. Cook patties on both sides for at least 2 minutes each or until all sides turn brown. Remove tray of muffins from oven. Place cooked sausage patties on top of the cheese on muffins. Return tray to the oven.

In the same pan, position onion rings flat into a single layer. Crack one egg inside each of the onion rings to make them round. Add water carefully into the sides of the pan and cover. Cook for 2 minutes.

Remove tray of muffins from the oven. Add eggs on top of patties, then top with the other muffin half.

Serve warm.

Nutrition: Calories 453, Total Fat 15 g, Carbohydrates 67 g, Protein 15 g, Sodium 1008 mg

18.   Starbucks' Spinach and Feta Breakfast Wraps

Preparation Time: 5 minutes

Cooking Time: 20 minutes

Servings: 6

Ingredients

10 ounces spinach leaves

1 14½-ounce can dice tomatoes, drained

3 tablespoons cream cheese

10 egg whites

½ teaspoon oregano

½ teaspoon garlic salt

⅛ Teaspoon pepper

6 whole wheat tortillas

4 tablespoons feta cheese, crumbled

Cooking Spray

Directions

Apply light coating of cooking spray to a pan. Cook spinach leaves on medium-high heat for 5 minutes or until leaves wilt, then stir in tomatoes and cream cheese. Cook for an additional 5 minutes or until cheese is melted completely. Remove from pan and place into glass bowl and cover. Set aside.

In the same pan, add egg whites, oregano, salt, and pepper. Stir well and cook at least 5 minutes or until eggs are scrambled. Remove from heat.

Microwave tortillas until warm. Place egg whites, spinach and tomato mixture, and feta in the middle of the tortillas. Fold sides inwards, like a burrito.

Serve.

Nutrition: Calories 157, Total Fat 3 g, Carbohydrates 19 g, Protein 14 g, Sodium 305 mg

19.   Spinach and Cheese Egg Soufflé from Panera

Preparation Time: 15 minutes

Cooking Time: 25 minutes

Servings: 4

Ingredients

1 tube butter flake crescent rolls

6 eggs, divided

2 tablespoons milk

2 tablespoons heavy cream

¼ cup cheddar cheese, grated

¼ cup jack cheese, grated

1 tablespoon Parmesan cheese

3 tablespoons fresh spinach, mince

4 slices of bacon, cooked and crumbled

Cooking spray

¼ teaspoon salt

¼ cup Asiago cheese, grated, divided

Directions

Preheat oven to 375°F.

Add 5 eggs, milk, heavy cream, cheddar cheese, jack cheese, parmesan cheese, spinach, bacon, and salt to a nonreactive bowl. Mix well until combined then heat in microwave for about 30 seconds. Stir, then microwave for another 20 seconds. Repeat about 5 times or until egg mixture is a bit thicker but still runny and uncooked. Roll out crescent roll dough. Make 4 rectangles by pressing together the triangles. Then, using a roll pin, stretch them out until they are 6in x 6in square. Coat ramekin with cooking spray and place flattened roll inside, making sure the edges are outside the ramekin. Add ⅓ cup egg mixture and then about ⅛ cup Asiago cheese. Wrap edges of the roll-on top. Repeat for remaining rolls. Whisk remaining egg with salt lightly in a bowl then, with a pastry brush, brush on top of each crescent roll dough. Place ramekins in the oven and bake for 20 minutes or until brown.

Serve.

Nutrition: calories 303, total fat 25 g, saturated fat 11 g, Carbohydrates 4 g, sugar 1 g, fibers 0 g, protein 20 g, sodium 749 mg

20. IHOP's Healthy "Harvest Grain 'N Nut" Pancakes

Preparation Time: 5 minutes

Cooking Time: 5 minutes

Servings: 4

Ingredients

1 teaspoon olive oil - ¾ cup oats, powdered

¾ cup whole wheat flour - 2 teaspoons baking soda

1 teaspoon baking powder - ½ teaspoon salt

1½ cup buttermilk

¼ cup vegetable oil

1 egg

¼ cup sugar

3 tablespoons almonds, finely sliced

3 tablespoons walnuts, sliced

Syrup for serving

Directions

Heat oil in a pan over medium heat.

As pan preheats, pulverize oats in a blender until powdered. Then, add to a large bowl with flour, baking soda, baking powder and salt. Mix well.

Add buttermilk, oil, egg, and sugar in a separate bowl. Mix with an electric mixer until creamy.

Mix in wet ingredients with dry ingredients, then add nuts. Mix everything together with electric mixer.

Scoop ⅓ cup of batter and cook in the hot pan for at least 2 minutes or until both sides turn golden brown. Transfer onto a plate, then repeat for the remaining batter.

Serve with syrup.

Nutrition: Calories 433, Total Fat 24 g, Carbohydrates: 46 g, Protein 12 g, Sodium 1128 mg

21.   Hash Brown Casserole

Preparation Time: 10 minutes

Cooking time: 55 minutes

Servings: 4–6

INGREDIENTS

1 (30-ounce) bag frozen hash browns, thawed

½ cup butter, melted

1 can cream of chicken soup

1 small onion, chopped

1-pound cheddar cheese, shredded (divided)

1 teaspoon salt

½ teaspoon black pepper

1 cup sour cream

DIRECTIONS

Preheat oven to 350°F.

Prepare a baking dish either by greasing the sides or spraying with nonstick cooking spray.

Mix together the onion, cream of chicken soup, pepper and all but 1 cup of the shredded cheese in a large bowl. When combined, mix in the sour cream until it is well incorporated.

Add the melted butter and hash browns. Stir to combine. Pour into the greased baking dish.

Bake for 45 minutes or until bubbly, then sprinkle the remaining cheese on top and bake until the cheese is melted

NUTRITION: total 26g, calories 221, fiber 12g, protein 8g

22.   **Cracker Barrel's Biscuits**

Preparation Time: 15 minutes

Cooking Time: 8 minutes

Servings: 8

Ingredients:

2 cups self-rising flour

⅓ Cup shortening

⅔ Cup buttermilk

Melted butter, to brush

Directions:

Preheat oven to 450 °F.

In a bowl, blend flour and shortening until blend is free and brittle. Pour in buttermilk. Blend well. Sprinkle flour onto a smooth surface and smooth mixture on beat. Cut batter into wanted shapes utilizing bread cutters. Arrange onto a preparing sheet. Put in broiler and cook for 8 minutes. Apply dissolved butter on best employing a brush. Serve.

Nutrition: Calories: 194 Fat: 9 g Carbohydrates: 24 g Protein: 4 g Sodium: 418 mg

23. Sonic's Supersonic™ Burrito

Preparation Time: 10 minutes

Cooking Time: 25 minutes

Servings: 8

Ingredients: 50 tater tots, frozen

1-pound breakfast sausage patties - 8 large eggs, beaten

2 tablespoons half and half - Salt and pepper, to taste

1 tablespoon butter - 8 6-inch flour tortillas

1½ cups cheddar cheese, grated - .1 medium onion, diced

½ cup pickled jalapeño peppers, sliced - 3 roma tomatoes, sliced

Salsa

Directions:

Cook tater tots per instructions on the package but cook them so they are a bit crispy. Set aside. In a pan, cook sausage patties. Break apart into large clumps until brown.

Mix eggs, salt, and pepper. Whisk until well mixed.

Cook butter in a frying pan over medium warm. Pour egg mixture and stir every now and then until scrambled remove from heat.

Microwave tortillas until warm but still soft. Then, in a vertical line in the center, add cheddar cheese, eggs, cooked sausage, tater tots, onions, jalapeños, and tomato. Fold the ingredients using the outer flaps of the tortilla. Repeat with remaining ingredients and tortillas.

Serve warm with salsa.

Nutrition: Calories: 636 Fat: 40 g Saturated Fat: 16 g Carbohydrates: 39 g Sugar: 4 g Fibers: 3 g Protein: 28 g Sodium: 1381 mg

Chapter 3:
Appetizers Recipe

24.   White Spinach Queso

Preparation Time: 5 minutes

Cooking Time: 10 minutes

Servings: 12

Ingredients:

2 tablespoons flour

8 ounces white American cheese

2 cups baby spinach leaves, fresh

¾ cup whole milk

2 tablespoons butter

½ teaspoon garlic powder

2 cups Jack cheese

1 tablespoon canola oil

Optional Ingredients:

Queso fresco crumbles

Pico de Gallo salsa

Guacamole

Directions:

Set your oven to broil. Now, over medium high heat in a large, cast iron skillet; heat the canola oil until hot. Add and cook the spinach until just wilted; immediately remove from the hot pan.

Add butter to the hot pan and then add the flour, stir well & cook for a few seconds then slowly add the milk.

Add in the garlic powder; whisk well then add the cheeses.

Continue to stir the mixture until thick & bubbly, for a minute or two and then, add in the spinach leaves; stir well.

Broil until the top turn golden brown, for a couple of minutes.

Top with salsa, guacamole and queso; serve immediately & enjoy.

Nutrition: Calories: 459 Fat: 15 g Carbohydrates: 67 g Protein: 15 g Sodium: 1008 mg

25.   Awesome Blossom Petals

Preparation Time:15 minutes

Cooking Time: 15 minutes

Servings: 6

Ingredients:

For Seasoned Breading:

¼ teaspoon onion powder

2 ½ cups flour

½ teaspoon ground black pepper

2 teaspoons seasoned salt

½ teaspoon paprika

1 cup buttermilk

¼ teaspoon garlic powder

For Blossom Sauce:

1/8 teaspoon cayenne pepper

2 tablespoons ketchup

½ cup sour cream

1 ½ teaspoons prepared horseradish

½ teaspoon seasoned salt

Other ingredients

Vegetable oil for frying

Directions:

For Blossom Sauce:

Combine the sour cream with ketchup, horseradish, cayenne pepper and seasoned salt in a small bowl; stir the ingredients well. Cover & let chill in a refrigerator until ready to serve.

For Onion:

Peel the onion.

Cut the stem of the onion off; place it on the cutting board, stem side down. Cut the onion horizontally and vertically into half then make two more diagonal cuts.

For Breading:

Add buttermilk in a large bowl.

Combine flour together with garlic powder, black pepper, paprika, onion powder and seasoned salt in a separate bowl. Using a large fork; give the ingredients a good stir until well mixed.

Put the onions first into the flour and then dip them into the buttermilk; then into the flour again. Let the onions to rest on the wire rack.

For Cooking:

Preheat oil until it reaches 350 F. Work in batches & add the onions into the hot oil (ensure that you don't overcrowd the onions); cook until turn golden brown, for 2 to 3 minutes.

Remove them from the hot oil & then place them on a wire rack to drain.

Serve hot & enjoy.

Nutrition: Calories: 158 Fat: 5 g Carbohydrates: 20 g Protein:17 g

26.   Olive Garden Paste e Fagioli

Preparation Time: 10 minutes

Cooking Time: 25 minutes

Servings: 8

Ingredients:

1 tablespoon of olive oil

1 lb. ground of sausage

2/3 cup of diced carrots

2/3 cup cut celery

2/3 cup white or yellow onion

4 garlic, chopped

1 can of dry great Northern beans

1 can red kidney beans, drained

1 cup drained ditalini pasta

2 boxes Chicken Broth

2 cans Organic Diced Tomatoes

¼ cup grated fresh Parmesan cheese

1 tablespoon fresh chopped parsley

Salt and pepper, to taste

Directions:

In a huge pot, heat olive oil over medium-high warmth. At the point when oil is hot, include hotdog, carrots, celery, onion and garlic to pot and cook, mixing once, until frankfurter is cooked through and onion and garlic have relaxed and get fragrant.

Include beans, pasta, stock and tomatoes. Mix until all around blended. Spread and cook for 15 minutes, or until pasta is still somewhat firm.

Salt and pepper to taste. Serve beat with Parmesan and new parsley

Nutrition: Calories: 345 Fat: 14 g Carbohydrates: 34 g Protein: 54 g Sodium: 1435 mg

27.   Texas Chili Fries

Preparation Time: 10 minutes

Cooking Time: 20 minutes

Servings: 4

Ingredients:

1 package of bacon

1 bag cheese blend, shredded

Ranch salad dressing

1 bag steak fries, frozen

1 jar jalapeno peppers

Directions:

Evenly spread the fries over a large-sized cookie sheet & bake as per the directions mentioned on the package.

Line strips of bacon on a separate cookie sheet & bake until crispy.

When the bacon and fries are done; remove them from the oven.

Add a thick layer of jalapenos and cheese; crumble the bacon over the fries.

Bake in the oven again until the cheese is completely melted.

Serve hot with some Ranch salad dressing on side and enjoy.

Nutrition: Calories: 537 Fat: 17 g Carbohydrates: 56 g Protein: 36 g Sodium: 683 mg

28.   Raspberry Lemonade

Preparation Time: 2 minutes

Cooking Time: 3 minutes

Servings: 8

Ingredients:

1 cup water

1 cup sugar

1 cup freshly squeezed lemon juice

1 ½ cups fresh

Directions:

In a pan, heat the water with sugar well until the sugar completely dissolves.

Meanwhile, purée the raspberries in a blender. Add the contents of the saucepan and the cup of lemon juice.

Wet the rim of your glass and dip it into a bit of sugar to coat the rim before pouring the lemonade into the glass.

Nutrition: Calories: 234 Fat: 56. 2 g Carbohydrates: 23. 8 g Protein: 23. 5 g Sodium: 1324 mg

29. Olive Garden's Creamy Zuppa Toscana

Preparation Time: 25 minutes

Cooking Time: 1 hour

Servings: 6

Ingredients

1-pound Italian sausage, ground

1¼ teaspoon red pepper flakes, ground

4 bacon slices, cut into ½-inch pieces

1 large onion, diced

1 tablespoon minced garlic

5 13¾-ounce cans chicken broth

6 potatoes, finely chopped

1 cup heavy cream

2 cups fresh spinach leaves

Directions

In a large pot, cook sausage and red pepper flakes on medium-high heat for at least 10 minutes or until brown. Drain. Transfer to a bowl and set aside.

In the same pot, cook bacon on medium heat for 10 minutes or until crunchy. Drain drippings until only a few tablespoons are left at the bottom of the pot. Mix in onions and garlic with the bacon. Cook for 5 minutes.

Put chicken broth into the pot and adjust heat to high. Bring to a boil. Add potatoes and boil for 20 minutes. Adjust heat to medium and mix in cream and cooked sausage to reheat.

Stir in spinach and serve.

Nutrition: Calories 554, Total Fat 33 g, Carbohydrates 46 g, Protein 20 g, Sodium 2386 mg

30.   tarbuck's Pumpkin Scones

Preparation Time: 25 minutes

Cooking Time: 15 minutes

Servings: 8

Ingredients:

Scones:

2 cups all-purpose flour

⅓ Cup brown sugar

1 teaspoon cinnamon

1 teaspoon baking powder

¾ teaspoon cloves, ground

½ teaspoon ginger, ground

½ teaspoon nutmeg, ground

½ teaspoon baking soda

¼ teaspoon salt

½ cup unsalted butter, cut into cubes (keep cold)

½ cup pumpkin puree

3 tablespoons milk

1 large egg

2 teaspoons vanilla extract

Flour, for rolling dough

Glaze:

1 cup powdered sugar

2 tablespoons milk

Spiced glaze:

1 cup powdered sugar

¼ teaspoon cinnamon

¼ teaspoon cloves, ground

¼ teaspoon ginger, ground

Pinch nutmeg

2 tablespoons milk

Directions:

Heat oven to 400°F and get ready a baking tray lined with parchment paper.

Mix flour, sugar, cinnamon, baking powder, cloves, ginger, nutmeg, baking soda, and salt in a bowl. Using your fingers, incorporate cold butter into the bowl until mixture is crumbly.

Stir together pumpkin puree, milk, egg, and vanilla in another bowl. Add to dry ingredients and mix until mixture becomes a soft dough.

Sprinkle a flat surface with flour. Transfer dough onto surface and knead for about 3 minutes. Flatten dough with a rolling pin into a large rectangle, about 1 inch thick and 10 by 7 inches. Cut in a cross to make 4 equal rectangles, then cut each rectangle diagonally. This makes 8 triangles.

Transfer dough onto baking tray, careful to keep triangles from touching. Bake for about 10 minutes or until baked through.

Prepare the glaze by mixing ingredients in a bowl until smooth. Repeat the step for the spiced glaze.

Allow scones to cool for about 10 minutes. Coat with glaze, then drip spiced glaze on top in zigzags.

Allow glazes to set before serving.

Nutrition: Calories 393 kcal Total Fat 12 g Carbohydrates 60 g Protein 6 g

31. Starbuck's Iced Vanilla Latte

Preparation Time: 5 minutes

Cooking Time: 0 minutes

Servings: 1

Ingredients:

2 cups strongly brewed coffee, cold

1/2 cup milk or cream

2 tablespoons vanilla syrup

1 cup ice

Directions:

Fill two glasses with ice. Mix together coffee, milk/cream, and vanilla syrup before pouring over ice. Serve immediately.

Nutrition: Calories: 111 Carbohydrates: 10g Protein: 2g Fat: 8g

32.   **Starbucks Graham Latte**

Preparation Time: 5 minutes

Cooking Time: 0 minutes

Servings: 1

Ingredients: 4 oz. milk - 4 oz. coffee

1/4 teaspoon vanilla - 1/4 teaspoon of Honey

1/4 teaspoon of Cinnamon - Graham crackers

Mason jar

Directions:

In your coffee glass include your honey, vanilla and cinnamon. Brew a glass of your favorite coffee and pour into your mug. Mix gently. Using a Bricklayer jar pour in 1/2 glass of milk with the cover. Shake the drain enthusiastically and expel the top. Place within the microwave for 45 seconds. Slowly pour milk into your coffee. Using a spoon scoop the foam onto your coffee. Place 3-4 Graham wafers in a Ziploc pack and pulverize them. Sprinkle the wafers on best of your coffee.

Nutrition: Calories: 80kcal Carbohydrates: 7g Protein: 4g Fat: 4g Fiber: 1g Sugars: 7g

33.   Starbucks Eggnog Latte

Preparation Time: 5 minutes

Cooking Time: 0 minutes

Servings: 1

Ingredients:

4 ounces boiling water

1 to 2 teaspoons instant espresso powder

1/4 cup milk

1/2 cup eggnog

1 teaspoon vanilla extract

1/2 tablespoon light brown sugar

1/8 teaspoon ground cinnamon

Pinch of nutmeg, or to taste, plus more for dusting

Whipped cream, optional

Directions:

Mix the coffee powder into the hot water and set aside. In a glass measuring glass combine milk, eggnog, vanilla, brown sugar, cinnamon and nutmeg; whisk/stir until completely combined. Place in Microwave and cook for 1 minute and 30 seconds, or until the milk begins to foam up. Remove from Microwave and stir/whisk once more. Place in Microwave for an extra 30 seconds, or until the milk starts to foam up once more. Remove and, whereas mixing the eggnog-mixture, gradually pour the coffee into the eggnog-. Blend. Top with whipped cream and clean with nutmeg. Serve.

Nutrition: Calories: 184 Fat: 7g Carbohydrates: 19g Sugar: 19g Protein: 7g

34.   Subway Ham Sandwich

Preparation Time: 10 minutes

Cooking Time: 5 minutes

Servings: 2

Ingredients:

Bread -

4 slices of cheese - halved

6 slices of Meat

1 tomato - sliced

6 lettuce leaves

6 slices of cucumber

1 small green bell pepper - sliced

Jalapenos/pickles/olives (optional)

2 tablespoons of sauce (mayonnaise/honey mustard/sweet onion/ranch)

Directions:

Plate the bread on a cutting board and cut it in half the long way. Once you've got opened up your bread, straighten it down so that it remains open. Place the cuts of meat on one side of the bread. The sum of meat you put on is your inclination. Put the cheese cuts on beat of the layer of meat. At this point, if you prefer your sandwich toasted, you'll be able pop usually the broiler for 2 minutes. Put the vegetables on the other half of the bread. Best with pickles or olives, in case utilizing. Finish your sandwich with a pile tablespoon of sauce. Once more, the sum of sauce you put on your sandwich depends on your individual inclination. Bring the sandwich together and cut it into half and serve.

Nutrition: Calories: 290 Fat: 4.5g Carbohydrates: 46g Fiber: 5g Protein: 18g

35. Taco Bell Cheese Quesadillas

Preparation Time: 10 minutes

Cooking Time: 10 minutes

Servings: 6

Ingredients:

4 flour tortillas (8 inches), warmed

1-1/2 cups shredded Mexican cheese blend

1/2 cup salsa

Directions:

Put the tortillas on a greased heating sheet. Combine the cheese and salsa; spread over half of each tortilla. Overlay over. Broil 4 in. from the warm for 3 minutes on each side or until brilliant brown. Cut into wedges.

Nutrition: Calories: 223 Fat: 11g Carbohydrates: 21g Sugars: 1g Fiber: 1g Protein: 9g

36. Panda Express's Cream Cheese Rangoon

Preparation Time: 5 minutes

Cooking Time: 5 minutes

Servings: 24 minutes

Ingredients:

¼ cup green onions, chopped

½ pound cream cheese, softened

½ teaspoon garlic powder

½ teaspoon salt

24 wonton wrappers

Oil for frying

Directions:

Add the green onions, cream cheese, garlic powder and salt to a medium sized bowl and mix together.

Lay the wonton wrappers out and moisten the edges of the first one. Add about ½ tablespoon of filling to the center of the wrapper and seal by pinching the edges together, starting with the corners and working your way inward. Make sure it is sealed tightly. Repeat with the remaining wrappers.

Add about 3 inches of oil to a large pot. Heat it to about 350°F, then add the wontons a few at a time and cook until brown.

Remove from oil and place on a paper-towel-lined plate to drain.

Nutrition: Calories: 193 Fat: 5 g Carbohydrates: 100 g Protein: 11 g Sodium: 123 g

37. PF Chang's Hot and Sour Soup

Preparation Time: 10 minutes

Cooking Time: 10 minutes

Servings: 4-6

Ingredients:

6 ounces chicken breasts, cut into thin strips

1-quart chicken stock

1 cup soy sauce

1 teaspoon white pepper

1 (6 ounce) can bamboo shoots, cut into strips

6 ounces wood ear mushrooms, cut into strips or canned straw mushrooms, if wood ear can't be found

½ cup cornstarch

½ cup water

2 eggs, beaten

½ cup white vinegar

6 ounces silken tofu, cut into strips

Sliced green onions for garnish

Directions:

In a nourishment processor or blender, finely mince ½ pound of the shrimp. Dice the other ½ pound of shrimp. In a blending bowl, combine both the minced and diced shrimp with the remaining fixings. Spoon around 1 teaspoon of the blend into each wonton wrapper. Damp the edges of the wrapper together with your finger, at that point overlap up and seal firmly. Cover and refrigerate for at slightest an hour. In a medium bowl, combine all of the fixings for the sauce and mix until well combined. When prepared to serve, bubble water in a saucepan and cover with a steamer. You will need to gently oil the steamer to keep the dumplings from staying. Steam the dumplings for 7–10 minutes. Serve with sauce.

Nutrition: Calories: 345 Fat: 1.2 g Carbohydrates: 2.2 g Protein: 23.3 g Sodium: 145

38. Pei Wei 's Thai Chicken Satay

Preparation Time: 20 minutes

Cooking Time: 10-20 minutes + Marinating Time: 20 minutes

Servings: 2-4

Ingredients:

1-pound boneless, skinless chicken thighs

6-inch bamboo skewers, soaked in water

Thai satay marinade

1 tablespoon coriander seeds

1 teaspoon cumin seeds

2 teaspoons chopped lemongrass

1 teaspoon salt

1 teaspoon turmeric powder

¼ teaspoon roasted chili

½ cup coconut milk

1½ tablespoons light brown sugar

1 teaspoon lime juice

2 teaspoons fish sauce

Peanut sauce

2 tablespoons soy sauce

1 tablespoon rice wine vinegar

2 tablespoons brown sugar

¼ cup peanut butter

1 teaspoon chipotle Tabasco

Thai sweet cucumber relish

¼ cup white vinegar

¾ cup sugar

¾ cup water

1 tablespoon ginger, minced

1 Thai red chili, minced

1 medium cucumber

1 tablespoon toasted peanuts, chopped

Directions:

Cut any excess fat from the chicken, then cut into strips about 3 inches long and 1 inch wide. Thread the strips onto the skewers.

Prepare the Thai Satay Marinade and the Peanut Sauce in separate bowls by simply whisking together all of the ingredients for each.

Dip the chicken skewers in the Thai Satay Marinade and allow to marinate for at least 4 hours. Reserve the marinade when you remove the chicken skewers.

You can either cook the skewers on the grill, basting with the marinade halfway through, or you can do the same in a 350-degree F oven. They taste better on the grill.

To prepare the Cucumber Relish, simply add all of the ingredients together and stir to make sure the cucumber is coated.

When the chicken skewers are done cooking, serve with peanut sauce and the cucumber relish.

Nutrition: Calories: 298 Fat: 5.4 g Carbohydrates: 7.5 g Protein: 61g Sodium: 190 g

39. Applebee's Baja Potato Boats

Preparation Time: 10 minutes

Cooking Time: 30 minutes

Servings: 4

Ingredients:

For Pico de Gallo: 1 ½ teaspoon fresh cilantro, minced

1 tablespoon canned jalapeño slices (nacho slices), diced

3 tablespoons Spanish onion, chopped

1 chopped tomato (approximately ½ cup)

A dash each of freshly-ground black pepper & salt

For the Potato Boats:

2 slices Canadian bacon diced (roughly 2 tablespoons)

Canola oil nonstick cooking spray, as required

⅓ Cup Cheddar cheese, shredded

3 russet potatoes, medium

⅓ Cup Mozzarella cheese

salt as needed

On the Side: - Salsa & sour cream

Directions:

Combine the entire Pico De Gallo ingredients together in a large bowl; mix well. When done, place in a refrigerator until ready to use.

Preheat your oven to 400 F in advance. Place potatoes in oven & bake until tender, for an hour. Set aside at room temperature until easy to handle. When done, cut them lengthwise 2 times. This should make 3 ½ to ¾" slices, throwing the middle slices away.

Increase your oven's temperature to 450 F. Take a spoon & scoop out the inside of the potato skins. Ensure that you must leave at least ¼ of an inch of the potato inside each skin. Spray the potato skin completely on all sides with the spray of nonstick canola oil. Put the skins, cut-side facing up on a large-sized cookie sheet. Sprinkle them with salt & bake in the preheated oven until the edges start to turn brown, for 12 to 15 minutes.

Combine both the cheeses together in a large bowl. Sprinkle approximately 1 ½ tablespoons of the mixture on each potato skin. Then sprinkle a teaspoon of the Canadian bacon over the cheese. Top this with a large tablespoon of the pico de gallo and then sprinkle each skin with some more of cheese.

Place the skins into the oven again & bake until the cheese melts, for 2 to 4 more minutes. Remove & let them sit for a minute. Slice each one lengthwise using a sharp knife. Serve hot with some salsa and sour cream on the side.

Nutrition: Calories: 254 Fat: 24 g Carbohydrates: 43 g Protein: 55 g Sodium: 779 mg

40.   Applebee's Chicken Wings

Preparation Time: 15 minutes

Cooking Time: 35 minutes

Servings: 6

Ingredients:

35 chicken wings

1 ½ tablespoon flour

3 tablespoons vinegar

1 ¼ teaspoon cayenne pepper

1 tablespoon Worcestershire sauce

12 ounces Louisiana hot sauce

¼ teaspoon garlic powder

Directions:

Cook the chicken wings either by deep-frying or baking.

Mix the entire sauce ingredients (except the flour) together over low-medium heat in a large saucepan. Cook until warm and then add in the flour; stir well until you get your desired level of thickness.

When thick; cover the bottom of 9x13" baking dish with the sauce. Combine the leftover sauce with the cooked wings & place them in the baking dish. Bake until warm, at 300 F.

Serve with blue-cheese dressing and celery sticks. Enjoy.

Nutrition: Calories: 189 Fat: 11 g Carbohydrates: 35 g Protein: 46 g Sodium: 2316 g

41.   Chicken Mushroom Soup

Preparation Time: 10 minutes

Cooking Time: 4 hours & 10 minutes

Servings: 4

Ingredients

½ cup All-purpose flour

5 boneless & skinless chicken breasts, cubed

½ small onion, diced

3 cups mushrooms, sliced

¼ cup carrots, diced

6 cups chicken Broth

¼ cup softened butter, at room temperature

3 cups heavy cream

½ teaspoon white pepper

1 teaspoon lemon juice, freshly squeezed

¼ teaspoon dried thyme

Ground black pepper & kosher salt, to taste

⅛ Teaspoon dried tarragon

Directions

Over medium heat in a large pot; heat the butter until completely melted and then toss in the onion, chicken, mushrooms & carrots. Sauté until the chicken is cooked through; cover the ingredients with the all-purpose flour.

Pour in the chicken broth, white pepper, thyme, tarragon, pepper & salt. Bring the blend to a stew & cook for 10 to 12 minutes.

Add the lemon juice and heavy cream. Let simmer again for 10 to 12 more minutes.

Serve hot & enjoy.

Nutrition: Calories: 630 Carbohydrates: 67g Fat: 16g Protein: 53g.

42.   Santa Fe Crispers Salad

Preparation Time: 10 minutes

Cooking Time: 30 minutes

Servings: 4

Ingredients

1 ½ pounds boneless skinless chicken breasts

1 tablespoon fresh cilantro, chopped

¾ cup Lawry's Santa Fe Chili Marinated with Lime and Garlic, divided

1 package (10 ounces) torn romaine lettuce, approximately 8 cups

2 tablespoons milk

1 cup black beans, drained and rinsed

½ cup sour cream

1 cup drained canned whole kernel corn

¼ cup red onion, chopped

1 medium avocado, cut into chunks

½ cup Monterey Jack, shredded

1 medium tomato, cut into chunks

Directions

Put chicken in a re-sealable marinade plastic bag

Add approximately ½ cup of the Santa Fe marinade, turn several times until nicely coated. Refrigerate for 30 minutes or longer. Removed the chicken from marinade; get rid of the leftover marinade

Grill the chicken until cooked through, for 6 to 7 minutes per side, over medium heat; brushing with 2 tablespoons of the leftover marinade

Cut the chicken into thin slices.

Combine the sour cream together with milk, leftover marinade and cilantro with wire whisk in medium-sized bowl until smooth

Arrange lettuce on large serving platter

Top with the chicken, avocado, corn, beans, cheese, tomato and onion.

Serve with tortilla chips and dressing. Enjoy.

Nutrition: Total fat 69g Carbohydrates 50g Fiber 10g Protein 33g Calories 165

43.   Caribbean Shrimp Salad

Preparation Time: 20 minutes

Cooking Time: 55 minutes

Servings: 4

Ingredients

8 cups baby spinach, fresh

¼ cup lime juice, freshly squeezed

2 tablespoons chili garlic sauce

½ teaspoon paprika

4 cups cooked shrimp, chopped (approximately 1 ½ pounds)

1 tablespoon grated lime rind

5 tablespoons seasoned rice vinegar, divided

½ teaspoon ground cumin

1 cup peeled mango, chopped

½ cup green onions, thinly sliced

2 garlic cloves, minced

1 cup radishes, julienne-cut

¼ cup peeled avocado, diced

2 tablespoons pumpkinseed kernels, unsalted

1 ½ tablespoons olive oil

Dash of salt

Directions

In a huge bowl; combine the cooked shrimp along with chili garlic sauce & 2 tablespoons of vinegar; hurl well. Cover & let chill for a hour.

Now, in a small bowl; combine the leftover vinegar together with garlic cloves, oil, lime juice, lime rind, ground cumin, paprika & salt; stirring well with a whisk.

Place 2 cups of spinach on each of 4 plates; top each serving with a cup of the prepared shrimp mixture. Arrange ¼ cup radishes, ¼ cup mango & 1 tablespoon of the avocado around the shrimp on each plate. Top each serving with approximately 1 ½ teaspoons of pumpkinseed kernels & 2 tablespoons of green onions. Drizzle each salad with approximately 2 tablespoons of the vinaigrette. Serve and enjoy.

Nutrition: Carbohydrates 26g Fiber 2g Fat 8g Calories 206

Chapter 4:
Lunch Recipes

44. Make-At-Home KFC Original Fried Chicken Dinner

Preparation Time: 20 minutes

Cooking Time: 40 minutes

Servings: 4

INGREDIENTS

Spice mix:

1 tablespoon paprika

2 teaspoons onion salt

1 teaspoon chili powder

1 teaspoon black pepper, ground

½ teaspoon celery salt

½ teaspoon dried sage

½ teaspoon garlic powder

½ teaspoon allspice, ground

½ teaspoon dried oregano

½ teaspoon dried basil

½ teaspoon dried marjoram

1 whole chicken, cut into parts

2 quarts frying oil

1 egg white - 1 ½ cups all-purpose flour

1 tablespoon brown sugar

1 tablespoon kosher salt

DIRECTIONS

Preheat oil in deep fryer to 350°F.

In a bowl, mix together ingredients for the spice mix. Then, add flour, sugar, and salt. Mix well until fully blended.

Coat each chicken piece with egg white, then the flour breading. Make sure that the chicken pieces are well-coated.

Exchange to a plate and permit chicken to dry for around 5 minutes.

Deep-fry breasts and wings together for about 12 minutes or until the temperature on a meat thermometer inserted in the breast's thickest part reads 165 °F. Do the same with legs and thighs. Usually these parts take 1-2 minutes more to cook.

Transfer pieces onto a plate lined with paper towels.

Serve.

NUTRITION: Calories 418Total Fat 22 G Carbohydrates 41 G Protein 15 G Sodium 1495 Mg

45.   Taco Bell Chicken Burrito

Preparation Time: 20 minutes

Cooking Time: 35 minutes

Servings: 6

Ingredients:

6 tablespoons butter - 1 large onion, chopped

1/4 cup chopped green pepper

1/2 cup all-purpose flour - 3 cups chicken broth

1 can diced tomatoes and green chilies

1 teaspoon ground cumin - 1 teaspoon chili powder

1/2 teaspoon garlic powder - 1/2 teaspoon salt

2 tablespoons chopped jalapeno pepper, optional

1 can (15 ounces) chili with beans

1 package (8 ounces) cream cheese, cubed

8 cups cubed cooked chicken

24 flour tortillas (6 inches), warmed

6 cups shredded Colby-Monterey Jack cheese

Salsa, optional

Directions:

Preheat oven to 350°. In a Dutch stove, warm butter over medium-high warm. Include onion and pepper; cook and blend until delicate. Blend in flour until mixed; slowly mix in broth. Bring to a bubble; cook and blend 2 minutes. Diminish warm; blend in tomatoes, seasonings and, in the event that craved, jalapeno. Cook 5 minutes. Include chili and cream cheese; blend until cream cheese is softened. Blend in chicken. Spoon almost 1/2 glass filling over center of each tortilla; sprinkle each with 1/4 container Colby-Monterey Jack cheese. Overlay foot and sides over filling and roll up. Put in 2 lubed 13x9-in. heating dishes. Bake, secured, 35-40 minutes or until warmed through. In case wanted, serve with salsa. Freeze alternative: Cool unbaked casseroles; cover and solidify. To utilize, in part defrost in fridge overnight. Evacuate from fridge 30 minutes some time recently preparing. Preheat stove to 350°. Cover casserole with thwart; heat as coordinated, expanding heating time to 50-55 minutes or until warmed through and a thermometer embedded in center peruses 160°.

Nutrition: Calories: 760 Fats: 44g Carbohydrates: 40g Sugars: 2g Fiber: 2g Protein: 51g

46.   **Chicken McNuggets**

Preparation Time: 25 minutes

Cooking Time: 15 minutes

Servings: 1

Ingredients:

Vegetable oil - 1 egg - 1 cup water

2/3 cup all-purpose flour - 1/3 cup tempura mix

2 teaspoons salt - 1 teaspoon onion powder

1/2 teaspoon Accent® - 1/4 teaspoon pepper

1/8 teaspoon garlic powder

4 chicken breast filets

Directions:

Beat the egg and after that combine it with 1 glass water in a little, shallow bowl. Blend. Combine the powder ingredients in a one-gallon estimate Zip Loc® sack. Smack each of the breast filets with a hammer until almost 1/4 inch thick. Trim each breast filet into chomp measured pieces. Coat each piece with the flour blend by shaking within the Zip Loc® pack. Remove and dig each piece within the egg blend, coating well. At that point return each nugget to the flour/seasoning blend. Shake to coat. Put chunks, pack and all, within the cooler for at slightest an hour. Cover and refrigerate remaining egg blend. After solidifying, rehash the "coating" prepare. Preheat broiler and expansive cookie sheet to 375°

Profound sear the chicken McNuggets™ at 375° for 10-12 minutes or until light brown and firm. (Cook as it were around 9 at a time) Drain on paper towels 3-5 minutes. Place deep-fried pieces on preheated cookie sheet in broiler and heat another 5-7 minutes. Serve together with your favorite McDonald's plunging sauce

Nutrition: Calories: 302 Fat: 20g Carbohydrates: 15g Sugar: 0.1g Protein: 16g

47.   Deep Fried Catfish

Preparation Time: 15 minutes

Cooking Time: 18 minutes

Servings: 4

Ingredients

Batter - 1 cup all-purpose flour - 1 cup cornmeal

1 tablespoon baking powder - 1 teaspoon salt

⅛ Teaspoon cayenne pepper

1 (12-ounce) bottle amber beer

Other ingredients

4 catfish fillets, about 6 ounces each - ½ teaspoon salt

½ teaspoon cracked black pepper

1 teaspoon garlic powder

Juice of one lemon - Lemon wedges, for serving

Peanut or vegetable oil for frying

Directions

Preheat the deep fryer to 350°F. To make the batter, combine the cornmeal, flour and baking powder and whisk well. Add the salt and cayenne pepper. Whisk until everything is well combined and slowly add in the beer, stirring well until you get a smooth mixture (about 2–3 minutes). Slice the catfish fillets in strips and season with salt and pepper. Sprinkle the garlic powder over the strips. Dredge each strip through the batter, ensuring both sides are evenly coated.

Fry in batches until golden brown, being careful not to overcrowd the fryer.

Drain the fillets on paper towels and season with salt and pepper and lemon juice.

Put on a serving platter and serve with lemon or lime wedges.

Nutrition: Calories 199, Total Fat 12g, Saturated Fat 6g, Carbohydrates 14g, Fiber 1g, Sugars 0g, Sodium 244mg, Protein 16g

48. Olive Garden's Zuppa Toscana Soup

Preparation time: 5 minutes

Cooking time: 40 minutes

Serving: 6

Ingredients

1 large head of cauliflower

1-pound sausage

3 cups kale leaves, chopped

1 medium white onion, peeled, chopped

1 ½ tablespoon minced garlic

½ teaspoon salt

½ teaspoon red pepper flakes

¼ teaspoon ground black pepper

4 cups of water

16 ounces chicken broth

1 cup heavy cream

Directions

Take a large pot, place it over medium-high heat and when hot, add sausage, crumble it, and then cook for 10 to 15 minutes until brown.

Add garlic and onion, stir until mixed, cook for 5 minutes, and then season salt, black pepper, and red pepper.

Switch heat to medium level, add florets, pour in water and chicken broth, stir and then cook for 20 minutes until florets have turned tender.

Then switch heat to the low level, add kale, pour in the cream, stir until combined, and then remove the pot from heat.

Ladle soup among six bowls and then serve.

Nutrition: 450 Cal; 37 g Fats; 18 g Protein; 12 g Net Carb; 3 g Fiber;

49. In N' Out Burger

Preparation time: 10 minutes

Cooking time: 10 minutes;

Serving: 5

Ingredients

For the Patties:

1 ½ pound ground beef

1 ½ teaspoon salt

1 teaspoon ground black pepper

5 slices of American cheese

For the Sauce:

1/3 cup mayonnaise

1 tablespoon ketchup, sugar-free

1 teaspoon mustard paste

2 tablespoons diced pickles

2 teaspoons pickle juice

½ teaspoon salt

½ teaspoon paprika

½ teaspoon garlic powder

For the Toppings:

10 slices of tomato

20 lettuce leaves

10 pickles slices

½ of large white onion, peeled, sliced thin

Directions

Prepare the sauce and for this, take a small bowl, place all of its ingredients in it, whisk until mixed; set aside until required.

Prepare the patties and for this, take a medium bowl, place beef in it, add salt and black pepper, stir until well combined, and then shape the mixture into ten balls.

Take a griddle pan, place it over high heat, grease it with oil and when hot, place meatball on it, press them down, and then cook 4 to 5 minutes per side until thoroughly cooked and browned.

When done, place a cheese slice on top of one patty, stack with another patty, and repeat with the remaining patties.

122 | P a g .

Assemble the burgers and for this, use two lettuce leaves as the bottom part of the bun, add some slices on onion, top with stacked burger patties, and then top with two slices of each tomato and pickles.

Drizzle the prepared sauce over patties, and then cover the top with two lettuce leaves.

Assemble the remaining burgers in the same manner and then serve.

Nutrition: 696 Calories; 49.5 g Fats; 52.2 g Protein; 6.5 g Net Carbohydrates; 4 g Fiber;

50.   Big Mac Bites

Preparation time: 15 minutes;

Cooking time: 15 minutes;

Serving: 16

Ingredients

For the Bites:

¼ cup diced white onion

1½ pounds ground beef

1 teaspoon salt

16 slices dill pickle

4 slices of American cheese

16 leaves of lettuce

For the Sauce:

4 tablespoon dill pickle relish

1 teaspoon onion powder

1 teaspoon garlic powder

1 teaspoon paprika

1 teaspoon white wine vinegar

2 tablespoon mustard paste

½ cup mayonnaise

Directions

Switch on the oven, then set it to 400 degrees F and let it preheat.

Meanwhile, prepare the bites and for this, take a large bowl, place beef in it, add onion and salt and then stir until well combined.

Shape the mixture into sixteen balls and then press down slightly to flatten balls into patties.

Arrange the patties into a large baking sheet lined with parchment sheet and then bake for 15 minutes until thoroughly cooked, turning halfway.

Meanwhile, prepare the sauce and for this, take a medium bowl, place all of its ingredients in it and then whisk until combined.

When patties have baked, remove the baking sheet from the oven and then drain the excess grease.

Assemble the bites and for this, cut each slice of American cheese into four squares, place each cheese square on top of each patty, return the baking sheet into the oven and wait until cheese melts.

Meanwhile, cut lettuce into squares and when the cheese melts, top each patty with lettuce squares and a slice of pickle and then secure the bite by inserting a skewer through it.

Serve the bite with prepared sauce.

Nutrition: 182 Cal; 12 g Fats; 10 g Protein; 0.6 g Net Carb; 0.4 g Fiber;

51. Longhorn's Parmesan Crusted Chicken

Preparation time: 10 minutes;

Cooking time: 30 minutes;

Serving: 4

Ingredients

4 chicken breasts, skinless

2 teaspoons salt

2 teaspoons ground black pepper

2 tablespoons avocado oil

For the Marinade:

1 tablespoon minced garlic

½ teaspoon ground black pepper

1 teaspoon lemon juice

3 tablespoon Worcestershire sauce

1 teaspoon white vinegar

½ cup avocado oil

½ cup ranch dressing

For the Parmesan Crust:

1 cup panko breadcrumbs

6 ounces parmesan cheese, chopped

5 tablespoons melted butter, unsalted

6 ounces provolone cheese, chopped

2 teaspoons garlic powder

6 tablespoons ranch salad dressing, low carb

Directions

Prepare the marinade and for this, take a small bowl, place all of its ingredients in it and then whisk until well combined.

Pound each chicken until ¾-inch thick, then season with salt and black pepper and transfer chicken pieces to a large plastic bag.

Pour in the prepared marinade, seal the bag, turn it upside to coat chicken with it and let it rest for a minimum of 30 minutes in the refrigerator.

Then take a large skillet pan, place it over medium-high heat, add oil and when hot, place marinated chicken breast in it and then cook for 5 minutes per side until chicken is no longer pink and nicely seared on all sides.

Transfer chicken to a plate and repeat with the remaining chicken pieces.

Meanwhile, switch on the oven, set it to 450 degrees F, and let it preheat.

When the chicken has cooked, prepare the parmesan crust and for this, take a small heatproof bowl, place both cheeses in it, pour in ranch dressing and milk, stir until mixed, and then microwave for 30 seconds.

Then stir the cheese mixture again until smooth and continue microwaving for another 15 seconds.

Stir the cheese mixture again, spread evenly on top of each chicken breast, arrange them in a baking sheet and then bake for 5 minutes until cheese has melted.

Meanwhile, take a small bowl, place breadcrumbs in it, stir in garlic powder and butter in it.

After 5 minutes of baking, spread the breadcrumbs mixture on top of the chicken and then continue baking for 2 minutes until the panko mixture turns light brown.

Serve chicken straight away with cauliflower mashed potatoes.

Nutrition: 557 Cal; 42 g Fats; 31 g Protein; 10 g Net Carb; 2 g Fiber;

52. Café Rio's Sweet Pork Barbacoa Salad

Preparation Time: 10 minutes

Cooking Time: 8 minutes

Servings: 8

Ingredients:

3 pounds pork loin

Garlic salt, to taste

1 can root beer

¼ cup water

¾ cup brown sugar

1 10-ounce can red enchilada sauce

1 4-ounce can green chilies

½ teaspoon chili powder

8 large burrito size tortillas

1½ serving Cilantro Lime Rice

1 can black beans, drained and heated

2 heads Romaine lettuce, shredded

1½ cups tortilla strips

1 cup Queso Fresco cheese

2 limes, cut in wedges

¼ cup cilantro

Dressing:

½ packet Hidden Valley Ranch Dressing Mix

1 cup mayonnaise

½ cup milk

½ cup cilantro leaves

¼ cup salsa verde

½ jalapeno pepper, deseeded

1 plump clove garlic

2 tablespoons fresh lime juice

Directions:

Sprinkle garlic salt on pork. Put in slow cooker with the fat side facing down. Add ¼ cup root beer and water. Cover and cook on low setting for 6 hours.

To prepare sauce add the rest of the root beer, brown sugar, enchilada sauce, green chilies, and chili powder in a blender. Blend until smooth.

Remove meat from slow cooker then transfer onto cutting board. Shred, discarding juices and fat. Return shredded pork to slow cooker with sauce. Cook on low setting for another 2 hours. When there is only about 15 to 20 minutes left to cook, remove lid to thicken sauce.

To prepare dressing mix all dressing ingredients in a blender. Puree until smooth. Then, transfer to refrigerator and allow to chill for at least 1 hour.

To assemble salad, layer tortilla, rice, beans, pork, lettuce, tortilla strips, cheese, and dressing in a bowl. Serve with a lime wedge and cilantro leaves.

Nutrition: Calories: 756 Fat: 28 g Saturated fat: 7 g Carbohydrates: 91 g Sugar: 31 g Fibers: 7 g Protein: 38 g Sodium: 1389 mg

53.   Spinach and Olives

Preparation Time: 5 minutes

Cooking Time: 20 minutes

Servings: 4

Ingredients:

½ cup tomato puree - 4 cups spinach; torn

2 cups black olives, pitted and halved

3 celery stalks; chopped. - 1 red bell pepper; chopped.

2 tomatoes; chopped. - Salt and black pepper to taste.

Directions:

Put spinach in a huge bowl; sprinkle with garlic powder and hurl. Put shrimp in a bowl; sprinkle with dark pepper and toss. Heat oil in a skillet over medium-high warm. Include shrimp; cook and mix until shinning pink on the exterior and the meat is dark, around 5 minutes. Include spinach, cook and blend until fair shriveled, approximately 1 minute.

Nutrition: Calories: 193; Fat: 6g; Fiber: 2g; Carbohydrates: 4g; Protein: 6g

54.   Courgette Casserole

Preparation Time: 7 minutes

Cooking Time: 20 minutes

Servings: 4

Ingredients:

14 oz. cherry tomatoes; cubed

2 spring onions; chopped.

3 garlic cloves; minced

2 courgette; sliced

2 celery sticks; sliced

1 yellow bell pepper; chopped.

½ cup mozzarella; shredded

1 tbsp. thyme; dried

1 tbsp. olive oil

1 tsp. smoked paprika

Directions:

Warm the oil in a huge broiling dish over a medium warm. Include the onion and cook for approximately 10 mins until relaxed and beginning to go brilliant brown. Include the garlic and cook for 5 mins more. Add the courgette and cook for almost 5 mins until beginning to relax. Tip within the tomatoes and provide everything a great mix. Stew for 35-40 mins or until tomatoes are decreased and courgettes soft, at that point mix within the basil and Parmesan.

Nutrition: Calories: 254; Fat: 12g; Fiber: 2g; Carbohydrates: 4g; Protein: 11g

55.　　Chicken and Asparagus

Preparation Time: 5 minutes

Cooking Time: 20 minutes

Servings: 4

Ingredients:

4 chicken breasts, skinless; boneless and halved

1 bunch asparagus; trimmed and halved

1 tbsp. olive oil

1 tbsp. sweet paprika

Salt and black pepper to taste.

Directions:

Begin by cooking the aromatics: I incorporate the regular onions, celery and carrots. Sauté those until they're fragrant and fork delicate but not as well soft. Add within the flavoring you're utilizing. I keep it straightforward with salt, pepper, garlic and oregano. Then include the tomatoes. I utilize a combination of diced canned tomatoes and tomato paste. Particle. But you'll too use fresh tomatoes and tomato sauce or any other variety to urge a tomato broth. Add vegetable broth, chicken broth or hamburger broth and bring to a boil. Finally include the cabbage and cook until the cabbage shrivels, around 20 minutes.

Nutrition: Calories: 230; Fat: 11g; Fiber: 3g; Carbohydrates: 5g; Protein: 12g

56.   Basil Chicken Bites

Preparation Time: 10 minutes

Cooking Time: 25 minutes

Servings: 4

Ingredients:

1 ½ lb. chicken breasts, skinless; boneless and cubed

½ cup chicken stock - ½ tsp. basil; dried

2 tsp. smoked paprika - Salt and black pepper to taste.

Directions: Combine ingredients in a huge bowl. Let marinate for 10 minutes. Heat oil in a deep-fryer or expansive pan to 400 degrees F (200 degrees C). Whisk egg in a little bowl until smooth. Pour tempura player blend into a moment little bowl. Plunge chicken pieces one at a time into the egg, at that point dig in tempura player blend, shaking off any abundance. Lower chicken pieces carefully into the hot oil in batches. Sear until chicken is brilliant brown, 5 to 8 minutes. Serve chicken sprinkled with basil leaves, green onions, white pepper, and salt.

Nutrition: Calories: 223; Fat: 12g; Fiber: 2g; Carbohydrates: 5g; Protein: 13g

57. BBQ Beef Brisket Sandwiches

Preparation Time: 15 minutes

Cooking Time: 9 hours and 5 minutes

Serving: 4

Ingredients

1 ½ lb. beef brisket

1 teaspoon celery salt

1 teaspoon of black pepper

½ cup Russian sauce

¾ teaspoon salt, or to taste

½ teaspoon garlic powder

½ teaspoon onion salt

1 teaspoon Worcestershire sauce

½ cup of barbecue sauce, walnut flavored

Directions

Combine celery salt, salt, black pepper, garlic, and onion salt in a clean small bowl; add Worcestershire sauce;

Spread the mixture over the ox breast; transfer to a slow cooker;

Cook over low heat until meat is tender, about 8 hours;

Transfer the cooked tender meat to a cutting board; shred in small pieces using two forks;

Measure ½ cup of the slow cooker in a saucepan. Mix Russian sauce and barbecue sauce; let it boil;

Combine the meat mixture and grated sauce in a slow cooker;

Cook over low heat until the flavors combine, about 1 hour.

Nutrition: Carbohydrates 36g Fat 4g Fiber 1g Calories 106

58. Mongolian Meat

Preparation Time: 10 minutes

Cooking Time: 15 minutes

Serving: 4

Ingredients

1 lb. flank steak - ¼ cup cornstarch

¼ cup canola oil - 2 teaspoons fresh ginger, chopped

1 tablespoon garlic, chopped

⅓ Cup soy sauce, low sodium - ⅓ Cup of water

½ cup dark brown sugar

4 green onion stalks, only green parts, cut into 2" pieces

Directions

Cut the flank steak against the grain (the grain is the length of the steak) along the ¼" reflection pieces and add it to a zippered pouch with cornstarch;

Press the steak into the bag, making sure that each piece is completely covered with cornstarch and let it rest;

Add canola oil to a considerable large skillet and heat over medium-high heat;

Add the steak, shaking off the excess cornstarch, to the pan in a single layer, and cook per side for 1 minute;

If you have to cook the steak in batches because your pan is not big enough, make it instead of cluttering it, you want to have a good grip on the steak and fill the pot with steam instead of burning; When the steak is cooked, remove it from the pan; Stir in chopped ginger and garlic to the pan and sauté for 10-15 seconds;

Add the water, soy sauce, and dark brown sugar to the pan and cook it to a boil; Add the steak and let the sauce thicken for 20 to 30 seconds; The corn starch we use in the steak should thicken the sauce. If you realize that it is not thickening enough, add 1 tablespoon of corn starch to 1 tablespoon of cold water and mix to break up the corn starch and include it to the skillet;

Add the green onion, stir to combine, and cook for nearly 20 to 30 seconds;

Serve fresh immediately.

Nutrition: calories 143 protein 26g total fat 3.5g carbohydrates 26 g

59.　Parmesan Chicken

Preparation Time: 25 minutes

Cooking Time: 35 minutes

Serving: 4

Ingredients

4 boneless, skinless chicken breast halves

Salt and black pepper to taste

2 eggs

1 cup panko breadcrumbs

½ cup of parmesan, grated

2 tablespoons of wheat flour

1 cup of cooking oil, for cooking

½ cup of tomato sauce

¼ cup fresh mozzarella, diced

¼ cup fresh basil, chopped

½ cup provolone cheese, grated

¼ cup of parmesan, grated

1 tablespoon of olive oil

Directions

Preheat an oven to 450° F;

The chicken breasts should be placed between two sheets of thick plastic (the resalable freezer bags work well) on a stable, level surface. Firmly grind the chicken with the smooth side of a meat mallet to a thickness of ½";

Season the chicken carefully with salt and pepper;

Beat the eggs in a considerable shallow bowl and set aside;

Mix breadcrumbs and ½ cup parmesan in another bowl, set aside;

Put the flour in a sieve; sprinkle over chicken breasts, evenly covering both sides;

Dip the floured chicken breast in the eggs, beaten;

Transfer the breast to the breadcrumb mixture by pressing the crumbs on both sides;

Repeat the procedure for each breast - reserve breaded chicken breasts for about 15 minutes;

Heat 1 cup of oil in a large skillet over medium-high heat until it begins to shine;

Cook the chicken until golden brown, about 2 minutes per side. The chicken will finish roasting;

Set the chicken in an ovenproof dish and decorate each breast with approximately ⅓ cup of tomato sauce;

Layer each chicken breast with equivalent measures of mozzarella cheese, fresh basil, and provolone cheese;

Sprinkle 1-2 tablespoons of Parmesan cheese on top and sprinkle with 1 tablespoon of olive oil;

Bake well in a preheated oven until the cheese is golden and bubbly, and the chicken breasts are no longer pink in color in the center, 15 to 20 minutes. An instant-read thermometer inserted in the center must read at least 165° F.

Nutrition: calories 205g protein 13.8g total fat 10g carbohydrates 28 g

60.   Chicken with Buttermilk

Preparation Time: 30 minutes

Cooking Time: 2 hours

Serving: 4

Difficulty Level: Intermediate

Ingredients

Marinade - ½ cup buttermilk

½ teaspoon of red pepper

¼ teaspoon of salt - ½ clove of garlic, chopped

Chicken - 2 lbs. of boneless, skinless chicken breast

⅓ Cup of wheat flour

1 tablespoon of cornstarch

½ teaspoon of dried thyme

½ teaspoon of paprika ground

Frying Oil

Directions

Set the chicken pieces in a large reusable food storage bag. Add all the ingredients for the marinade and refrigerate for at least 2 hours or overnight to marinate;

In a pie dish, mix the flour and all other chicken ingredients except oil. Heat about ½" of oil in a 12" skillet over medium-high heat;

Remove the chicken pieces from the marinade, some at a time, allowing the excess to drain;

Wrap the chicken in the flour mixture until it is well coated;

Add the chicken to the hot oil in a pan, a few pieces at a time, until all the pieces are in the pan. Carefully cover; Cook over medium-high heat for 10 minutes or until golden brown. Discard the marinade;

Discover the pot. Flip the chicken over;

Cook for 5 to 8 minutes more or until the chicken juice is obvious when the center of the thickest portion is cut (170° F for the breasts; 180° F for the thighs);

Drain the chicken over several layers of paper towels;

Serve hot or refrigerate and serve cold.

Nutrition: total fat 27g Carbohydrates 9g protein 29g Fats 4 g calories 225

Chapter 5:
Snack Recipes

61. Applebee's Triple Chocolate Meltdown

Preparation time: 25 min

Cooking time: 8 min

Servings: 2–3

Ingredients

4 ounces semisweet chocolate chips

½ cup butter

2 large whole eggs

2 large egg yolks

¼ cup sugar, plus more for dusting

2 tablespoons all-purpose flour

¼ teaspoon salt

Toppings

4 ounces white chocolate

4 ounces semisweet chocolate

2 teaspoons vegetable shortening, divided

4 scoops vanilla ice cream

Directions

Preheat oven to 400°F. Grease muffin pans or ramekins and dust with sugar. Melt chocolate chips with butter over a double boiler, whisking until smooth.

In a separate bowl, whisk together the whole eggs, yolks, and sugar until light and fluffy.

Whisk both mixtures together.

Gradually add flour and salt, whisking until blended.

Distribute evenly into prepared pans and arrange on a baking sheet.

Bake until edges are done, and centers are still soft (about 8 minutes).

Invert onto dessert plate.

Prepare toppings. Place each type of chocolate in separate, microwave-safe bowls. Add a teaspoon of shortening to each bowl. Microwave for about 15 seconds and stir. Repeat until smooth.

Top the cake pieces with ice cream and drizzle with melted chocolate.

Nutrition Calories 727, Total Fat 31 g, Carbohydrates 107 g, Protein 11 g, Sodium 562 mg

62.   BJ's Pizookie

Preparation time: 10 minutes

Cooking time: 10 minutes

Servings: 4

Ingredients

Nonstick cooking spray

1⅛ cups all-purpose flour

¼ teaspoon baking soda

½ teaspoon salt

½ cup (1 stick) butter or shortening

¼ cup brown sugar

½ cup granulated sugar

1 large egg, beaten

1 teaspoon vanilla

1 cup chocolate chips or chunks

3 scoops of vanilla ice cream

Directions

Preheat oven to 350°F. Grease a 9-inch round pan.

Filter to begin with 3 ingredients together in a bowl and set aside. Cream the butter and sugars. Add egg and vanilla, at that point beat until soft.

Add sifted dry ingredients and mix just to incorporate.

Stir in chocolate chips.

Spread dough evenly in pan.

Bake until edges are slightly browned and begin to separate from pan (about 10 minutes).

Serve with ice cream.

Nutrition: Calories 222, Total Fat 11.8 g, Carbohydrates 26.1g, Protein 2.8 g, Sodium 150 mg

63.   KFC's Chocolate Chip Cake

Preparation time: 10 minutes

Cooking time: 45 min

Servings: 10

Ingredients

1 (15¼-ounce) box devil's food cake mix

1 (3.4-ounce) package instant chocolate pudding

1 cup sour cream

4 eggs, beaten

½ cup water

½ cup canola oil

1½ cups chocolate chips

Cream Cheese Frosting

¼ cup unsalted butter, softened

4 ounces cream cheese, softened

3 cups powdered sugar

1 tablespoon milk

Directions

Preheat oven to 350°F. Grease and flour a Bundt cake pan.

In a huge bowl, blend cake and pudding blends together. Use an electric blender at moderate speed and include acrid cream, eggs, water, and oil until mixed.Use an electric mixer at slow speed and add sour cream, eggs, water, and oil until blended. Drop in chocolate chips and mix briefly to distribute.

Transfer to Bundt pan. Bake until toothpick inserted near the center comes out clean (about 45–50 minutes).

Leave in pan to cool for 20 minutes.

Remove from pan and place on a wire rack.

Prepare the frosting. Use a mixer to beat butter and cream cheese together until fluffy. Add the rest of the ingredients for frosting and beat 3–5 minutes longer. If too thick, add more milk drop by drop until the right consistency is achieved.

Pipe or drizzle the frosting over the top of the cooled cake. Let the frosting flow down the edges of the cake.

Nutrition: Calories 300, Total Fat 12 g, Carbohydrates 49 g, Protein 3 g, Sodium 190 mg

64.   McDonald's Apple Pie

Preparation time: 5 min

Cooking time: 30 min

Servings: 6

Ingredients

Oil, for frying

Powdered sugar, for dusting (optional)

Crust

1 cup unbleached all-purpose flour

½ teaspoon salt

1 teaspoon sugar

6 tablespoons butter

¼ cup ice water

Filling

2 medium apples, peeled, cored and diced

½ cup apple cider

¼ cup sugar

1 teaspoon cinnamon

1½ tablespoons lemon juice

⅛ teaspoon salt

2 tablespoons flour

Directions

Prepare the crust. Put flour, sugar and salt into a nourishment processor and beat a couple of times to blend. Add butter and beat to urge a coarse blend. Add water and beat fair until blend starts to follow and frame a mixture. Place on a floured surface and separate into 3 break even with parts.

Form each into a thick disc, wrap in plastic wrap and refrigerate until firm (about 30 minutes to 1 hour).

Prepare the filling. Place ingredients, except flour, in a saucepan and bring to a boil. Reduce heat and simmer until apples are tender (about 10–15 minutes). Stir in flour and cook until slightly thickened (about 1½ minutes). Remove from heat and let cool.

Roll out each third of the chilled dough over a floured surface to make 10-inch rectangles or ovals. Divide each into 2 to make 6 pieces.

Divide the filling into 6 and spoon into the center of each piece of dough.

Damp edges of the batter and overlap over. Press down edges with a fork to seal.

Deep fry in oil at 350°F, by batches, until golden brown (about 3 minutes on each side).

Drain on paper towels.

Clean with powdered sugar (in case utilizing) and serve.

Nutrition: Calories 250, Total Fat 13 g, Carbohydrates 32 g, Protein 2 g, Sodium 170 mg

65. Dunkin' Donuts Chocolate Munchkins

Preparation time: 10 min

Cooking time: 30 min

Servings: 30

Ingredients

2 tablespoons unsalted butter

1½ ounces unsweetened chocolate, roughly chopped

¼ cup buttermilk

1 tablespoon pure vanilla extract

1 large egg

1 cup all-purpose flour

¼ cup plus 2 tablespoons granulated sugar

¼ cup plus 2 tablespoons cocoa powder

¾ teaspoon baking powder

¼ teaspoon baking soda

½ teaspoon kosher salt

Vegetable oil, for deep frying

2 cups powdered sugar

2 tablespoons milk

2 teaspoons pure vanilla extract

Directions

To prepare dough, using a double boiler, heat butter and chocolate on top of saucepan with slightly simmering water on bottom until melted. Turn off heat, then set aside to cool. Pour in buttermilk and vanilla. Mix in egg. Whisk until combined.

Next, mix flour, sugar, cocoa powder, baking powder, baking soda, and salt in a large bowl. Pour liquid ingredients into bowl. Stir until mixed and dough forms. Remove from bowl and wrap in plastic wrap. Keep refrigerated for 30 minutes.

Preheat oil to 360° F 3-inches deep in a heavy bottomed pot.

Scoop out small pieces out of dough and form into balls using your hands. Deep fry only a few balls at a time so as to not overcrowd pot.

Cook balls for about 2 to 3 minutes until cooked through. Evacuate from oil employing a opened spoon, at that point organize onto a preparing plate lined with paper towels. Let cool.

As munchkins cool, make glaze by combining powdered sugar, milk, and vanilla in a bowl. Whisk until it forms a smooth consistency similar to heavy cream.

Glaze to coat with a fork or some tongs, raising it above glaze to let drip any excess. Transfer to a rack over a baking tray.

Serve once glaze dries.

Nutrition: Calories 97, Total Fat 4 g, Carbohydrates 15 g, Protein 1 g, Sodium 45 mg

66.   Maple Butter Blondie

Preparation Time: 15 minutes

Cooking Time: 35 minutes

Servings: 9

Ingredients:

⅓ Cup butter, melted - 1 cup brown sugar, packed

1 large egg, beaten - 1 tablespoon vanilla extract

½ teaspoon baking powder - ⅛ Teaspoon baking soda

⅛ Teaspoon salt

1 cup flour

⅔ cup white chocolate chips

⅓ Cup pecans, chopped (or walnuts)

Maple butter sauce

¾ cup maple syrup

½ cup butter

¾ cup brown sugar

8 ounces cream cheese

¼ cup pecans, chopped

Vanilla ice cream, for serving

Directions:

Preheat the oven to 350°F and coat a 9x9 baking pan with cooking spray.

In a mixing bowl, combine the butter, brown sugar, egg, and vanilla, and beat until smooth.

Filter within the heating powder, preparing pop, salt, and flour, and mix until it is well consolidated. Overlay within the white chocolate chips. Bake for 20–25 minutes. While those are within the broiler, plan the maple butter sauce by combining the maple syrup and butter in a medium pan. Cook over moo warm until the butter is dissolved. Add the brown sugar and cream cheese. Stir constantly until the cream cheese has completely melted, then remove the pot from the heat.

Remove the blondies from the oven and cut them into squares.

Top with vanilla ice cream, maple butter sauce, and chopped nuts.

Nutrition: Calories: 255 Fat: 65 g Carbohydrates: 67 g Protein: 18 g Sodium: 867 mg

67.   Baked Apple Dumplings

Preparation Time: 20 minutes

Cooking Time: 40 minutes

Servings: 2 to 4

Ingredients:

1 package frozen puff pastry

1 cup of sugar

6 tablespoons of breadcrumbs

2 teaspoons of ground cinnamon

1 pinch ground nutmeg

1 egg

4 apples

Vanilla ice cream

Icing

1 cup confectioners' sugar

1 teaspoon vanilla extract

3 tablespoons milk

Pecan Streusel

⅔ Cup chopped toasted pecans

⅔ Cup packed brown sugar

⅔ Cup all-purpose flour

5 tablespoons melted butter   Icing

1 cup confectioners' sugar

1 teaspoon vanilla extract

3 tablespoons milk

Pecan Streusel

⅔ Cup chopped toasted pecans

⅔ Cup packed brown sugar

⅔ Cup all-purpose flour

5 tablespoons melted butter

Directions:

Preheat the oven to 425°F.

When the puff cake has totally defrosted, roll out each sheet to degree 12 inches by 12 inches. Cut the sheets into quarters. Combine the sugar, breadcrumbs, cinnamon and nutmeg together in a little bowl. Brush one of the cake squares with a few of the beaten egg.

Include approximately 1 tablespoon of the breadcrumb blend on best, at that point include half an apple, center side down, over the scraps. Include another tablespoon of the breadcrumb blend. Seal the dumpling by pulling up the corners and squeezing the baked good together until the creases are completely fixed. Rehash this prepare with the remaining squares. Assemble the fixings for the pecan streusel in a little bowl. Grease a heating sheet, or line it with material paper. Put the dumplings on the sheet and brush them with a bit more of the beaten egg. Beat with the pecan streusel.

Prepare for 15 minutes, at that point diminish warm to 350°F and heat for 25 minutes more or until softly browned. Make the icing by combining the confectioners' sugar, vanilla and deplete until you reach the proper consistency. When the dumplings are done, let them cool to room temperature and sprinkle them with icing a few times as of late serving.

Nutrition: Calories: 145 Fat: 57 g Carbohydrates: 87 g Protein: 66.9 g Sodium: 529 mg

68.   Peach Cobbler

Preparation Time: 10 minutes

Cooking Time: 45 minutes

Servings: 4

Ingredients:

1¼ cups Bisquick

1 cup milk

½ cup melted butter

¼ teaspoon nutmeg

½ teaspoon cinnamon

Vanilla ice cream, for serving

Filling

1 (30-ounce) can peaches in syrup, drained

¼ cup sugar

Topping

½ cup brown sugar

¼ cup almond slices

½ teaspoon cinnamon

1 tablespoon melted butter

Directions:

Preheat the oven to 375°F.

Oil the foot and sides of an 8×8-inch container. Whisk together the Bisquick, drain, butter, nutmeg and cinnamon in a expansive blending bowl. When completely combined, pour into the lubed preparing container. Mix together the peaches and sugar in another blending bowl. Put the filling on best of the player within the dish. Heat for approximately 45 minutes. In another bowl, blend together the brown sugar, almonds, cinnamon, and liquefied butter. After the cobbler has cooked for 45 minutes, cover equitably with the topping and heat for an extra 10 minutes.

Nutrition: Calories: 168 Fat: 76 g Carbohydrates: 15 g Protein: 78.9 g Sodium: 436 mg

69.   Royal Dansk Butter Cookies

Preparation Time: 15 minutes

Cooking Time: 25 minutes

Servings: 10

Ingredients:

120g cake flour, sifted

½ teaspoon vanilla extract

25g powdered sugar

120g softened butter, at room temperature

A pinch of sea salt, approximately ¼ teaspoon

Directions:

With a hand mixer; mix the butter with sugar, vanilla & salt until almost doubled in mass & lightened to a yellowish-white in color, for 8 to 10 minutes, on low to middle speed.

Scrape the mixture from the sides of yours bowl using a rubber spatula. Sift the flour x 3 times & gently fold in until well incorporated.

Exchange the blend into a sheet of plastic wrap, roll into log & cut a hole on it; placing it into the piping bag attached with a nozzle flower tips 4.6cm/1.81" x 1.18".

Pipe each cookie into 5cm wide swirls on a parchment paper lined baking tray.

Cover & place them in a freezer until firm up, for 30 minutes.

Preheat your oven to 300 F in advance. Once done; bake until the edges start to turn golden, for 20 minutes.

Let completely cool on the cooling rack before serving.

Store them in an airtight container.

Nutrition: Calories: 455 Fat: 67 g Carbohydrates: 12. 8 g Protein: 66.3 g Sodium: 552 mg

70.   Banana Pudding

Preparation Time: 15 minutes

Cooking Time: 1 hour and 30 minutes

Servings: 8 to 10

Ingredients:

6 cups milk

5 eggs, beaten

¼ teaspoon vanilla extract

1⅛ cups flour

1½ cups sugar

¾ pound vanilla wafers

3 bananas, peeled

8 ounces Cool Whip or 2 cups of whipped cream

Directions:

In a huge pot, warm the milk to almost 170°F. Mix the eggs, vanilla, flour, and sugar together in a expansive bowl. Very gradually include the egg blend to the cautioned drain and cook until the blend thickens to a custard consistency.

Layer the vanilla wafers to cover the bottom of a baking pan or glass baking dish. You can also use individual portion dessert dish or glasses.

Layer banana slices over the top of the vanilla wafers. Be as liberal with the bananas as you want.

Layer the custard mixture on top of the wafers and bananas. Move the pan to the refrigerator and cool for 1½ hours. When ready to serve, spread Cool Whip (or real whipped cream, if you prefer) over the top. Garnish with banana slices and wafers if desired.

Nutrition: Calories: 166 Fat: 56 g Carbohydrates: 78.9 g Protein: 47.8 g Sodium: 578 mg

71.   McDonald's® McFlurry®

Preparation time: 15 minutes

Cooking Time: 15 minutes

Servings: 4

Ingredients

Vanilla Ice Cream,

Skim Milk

Butterfingers, M&M's, Oreos, Reese's, fudge brownies

Ice Cubes

Directions

Mix 2 cups vanilla ice cream with ¼ cup of skim milk; mix well but ensure you don't over mix

Now, get a cup & put 2 cups of vanilla ice cream, add Butterfingers, M&M's, Oreos, Reese's, fudge brownies & ¼ cup of milk; mix well. Add couple of ice cubes. Serve & enjoy!

Nutrition: Calorie: 340 kcal Fat: 11 g Carbohydrates: 53 g Sodium: 180 mg Protein: 8 g

72.   Hostess® Cupcakes

Preparation time: 15 minutes

Cooking Time: 1 hour 15 minutes

Servings: 10

Ingredients

For Cupcakes:

1 ½ cups sugar

2 cups flour

¾ cup Dutch process cocoa

1 teaspoon of baking powder

1 ½ teaspoons of baking soda

½ teaspoon salt

2 eggs

1 cup oil

¾ cup buttermilk

For Ganache:

¾ cup cream

7 ounces chocolate

For Filling:

4 tablespoons butter

1 cup powdered sugar

2 teaspoons vanilla

1 cup marshmallow crème

¾ cup hot coffee

1 teaspoon vanilla

For Icing:

½ stick butter

1 cup powdered sugar

½ teaspoon vanilla

½ -1 tablespoon milk

Directions

Preheat your oven to 350 F. Sift flour together with Dutch process cocoa, sugar, baking soda, baking powder & salt in a large sized bowl. Beat eggs together with oil, vanilla & buttermilk in a separate bowl, and then add the mixture into the dry ingredients. Beat in the warm coffee.

Pour the mixture into the lined muffin cups & fill them approximately 2/3 full; bake for 18 to 20 minutes at 350 F. Remove from oven & let cool a bit at room temperature. Beat all the filling ingredients together in a medium sized bowl. Fill a large sized piping bag. When you can easily handle the cupcakes, press their tip into the middle & squeeze one or two tablespoons of cream filling into the middle. Repeat the process for all the cupcakes.

Over medium heat settings in a large saucepan; heat the cream until the cream is hot & just begins to boil, stirring frequently. Transfer the cream immediately on top of the chocolate; whisk until smooth. Spread the slightly cooled but warm ganache on top of the filled cupcakes.

Whip all the icing ingredients together until smooth; if required, feel free to add more of milk. Fill a piping bag & pipe on the curls.

Nutrition: Calorie: 160 kcal Fat: 6 g Carbohydrates: 26 g Sodium: 210 mg Protein: 1 g

73.   7-Eleven Cherry Slurpee

Preparation time: 5 minutes

Cooking Time: 0 minutes

Servings: 5

Ingredients

3 cups club soda

1 cup sugar

1 teaspoon Kool-Aid cherry powdered drink mix

1 teaspoon maraschino cherry juice

2½ cups crushed ice

Fresh mint for serving

Directions

Combine all the ingredients in a blender.

Pulse for few minutes.

Serve chilled and top mint leaves, if desired.

Nutrition: Calories 151 Total fat 0 g Carbohydrates 40 g Protein 0 g Sodium 31 mg

74.   Pulled Pork Sandwich

Preparation Time: 45 minutes

Cooking Time: 6 hours

Servings: 4

Ingredients

Pork

6 tablespoons of paprika

3 tablespoons sugar, granulated

1 tablespoon of onion powder

Salt and black pepper, ground, to taste

1 (10-12 lbs.) boneless pork shoulder, washed and dried

12 sweet hamburger buns, cut in half

Coleslaw, to serve

Barbecue sauce

2 cups of ketchup

¼ cup lightly packaged brown sugar

¼ cup sugar, granulated

Black pepper, ground, to taste

1 ½ teaspoon onion powder, granulated

1 ½ teaspoon mustard powder

2 tablespoons lemon juice

2 tablespoons Worcestershire sauce

½ cup apple cider vinegar

2 tablespoons light corn syrup

Directions

If using a gas grill, preheat on one side;

Place the wood chips soaked in a smoking box. After smoking, reduce the heat to maintain a temperature of 275° F and grill the pork, covered, at the cooler side of the gas grill;

Combine the paprika, sugar and onion powder in a bowl;

Transfer 3 tablespoons of seasoning to a separate bowl, add 2 tablespoons of salt and 3 tablespoons of pepper and massage over the pork;

Carefully cover with plastic wrap and cool in a refrigerator for at least 2 hours or more (reserve the remaining barbecue seasoning);

Immerse 6 cups of wood chips in water, about 15 minutes, then drain. Do not immerse not too much; otherwise, the wood will go out of the fire;

Fill a smoker or kettle with charcoal and light. When the coals are becoming white, spread them out with tongs - spread ½ cup of wood chips over the grill coals (use 1 cup for grilling). The grill temperature should be around 275° F;

Set the fat pork face down on a grill in the smoker or on the grill;

Carefully cover and cook, turning the pork every hour or so until a thermometer inserted in the center records 165° F, about 6 hours in total;

While the pork is cooking, add more charcoal and wood chips to keep the temperature between 250° F and 275° F and maintain the smoke level;

Meanwhile, whisk the ketchup, 1 cup of water, the 2 sugars, 1 ½ teaspoons of pepper, onion and mustard powder, lemon juice, Worcestershire sauce, vinegar, syrup of corn and 1 tablespoon of barbecue seasoning reserved in a pan over high heat;

Heat to the point of boiling, stirring, then low the heat and cook, uncovered, occasionally stirring, at least 2 hours;

Transfer the pork to a roasting pan (you'll want to pick up all the delicious juices) and let it sit until its cold enough to handle;

Undo it in small pieces, stack it on a platter and pour the juice from the pan on top;

Mount the pork on the bottom of the cake, paint with a little barbecue sauce, top it with coleslaw and cover with the top cake. The best sandwich ever!

Nutrition: Carbohydrates 32 g. Dietary Fiber 1 g. Sugar 2 g. Fat 9 g. Calories 243

75.   Mud Pie

Preparation time: 30 minutes

Cooking Time: 15 minutes + cooling

Servings: 4

Ingredients

½ cup flour, all-purpose

½ cup chopped walnuts

¼ cup butter, softened

½ packet (3 oz.) of instant chocolate pudding mix

½ packet of cream cheese, softened

½ cup icing sugar

½ container (8 oz.) of frozen frosting

Pecans and grated chocolate, to serve

Directions

Set the oven's temperature to exactly 350° F;

In a suitably large bowl, beat the flour, nuts, and butter until well combined;

Press the bottom of a 13X9" baking tray. Cook until golden brown, about 15 minutes;

Remove on a wire rack. Cool completely;

Make chocolate pudding according to package directions; let it sit and stand for 5 minutes;

In a bowl, beat cream cheese and sugar until smooth. Mix 1 cup of beaten frosting;

Spread the prepared cream cheese mixture on the cooled crust;

Spread the pudding on the cream cheese layer;

Decorate with the rest of the beaten frosting;

Decorate with additional chocolate chips and nuts if desired.

Nutrition: Carbohydrates 70g Fat 20g Protein 6g Calories 146

Chapter 6:
Dinner Recipes

76.   Shrimp Scampi

Preparation Time: 10 minutes

Cooking Time: 30 minutes

Servings: 4

Ingredients:

1–2 pounds fresh shrimp, cleaned, deveined, and butterflied 1 cup milk

3 tablespoons olive oil

½ cup all-purpose flour

4 tablespoons Parmesan cheese, divided

¼ teaspoon salt

½ teaspoon fresh ground black pepper

¼ teaspoon cayenne pepper

6–8 whole garlic cloves

1 cup dry white wine

2 cups heavy cream

5–7 leaves fresh basil, cut into strips

1 diced tomato

2 tablespoons Parmesan cheese, finely grated

1 shallot, diced

1-pound angel hair pasta, cooked (hot)

Parsley, to garnish

Directions:

Put the shrimp in the milk and let it sit.

In a shallow bowl, combine the flour, 2 tablespoons of Parmesan, salt, pepper, and cayenne.

Pour the olive oil in a large skillet, making sure it's enough to cover the bottom. Heat over medium-high heat.

Take the shrimp from the milk and dredge in flour mixture. Transfer it to the skillet and cook about 2 minutes on each side. After the shrimp cooks, transfer it to a plate covered with a paper towel to drain.

Reduce the heat to medium-low and cook the garlic in the leftover oil. (Don't worry about any bits left from the shrimp because these will add flavor and help to thicken the sauce.)

After the garlic cooks for a couple of minutes, add the wine. Increase the heat and bring the mixture to a boil, then reduce the heat and simmer to reduce liquid to about half of the original volume.

Add the cream and simmer for about 10 more minutes, then add the basil, tomato, cheese, and shallots. Stir to combine.

Add the shrimp to the skillet and remove it from the heat.

Arrange the pasta on serving plates, topped with shrimp and covered with sauce. Garnish with parsley.

Nutrition: Calories: 454 Fat: 54 g Carbohydrates: 152 g Protein: 41 g Sodium: 1614 mg

77.   Red Beans and Rice from Popeye's

Preparation Time: 20 minutes

Cooking Time: 40 minutes

Servings: 10

Ingredients:

3 14-ounce cans red beans

¾ pounds smoked ham hock - 1¼ cups water

½ teaspoon onion powder - ½ teaspoon garlic salt

¼ teaspoon red pepper flakes - ½ teaspoon salt

3 tablespoons lard - Steamed long-grain rice

Directions:

Add 2 canned red beans, ham hock, and water to pot. Cook on medium heat and let simmer for about 1 hour.

Remove from heat and wait until meat is cool enough to handle. Then, remove meat from bone.

In a food processor, add meat, cooked red beans and water mixture, onion powder, garlic salt, red pepper, salt, and lard. Pulse for 4 seconds. You want the beans to be cut and the liquid thickened. Drain remaining 1 can red beans and add to food processor. Pulse for only 1 or 2 seconds.

Remove ingredients from food processor and transfer to the pot from earlier.

Cook on low heat, stirring frequently until mixture is heated through.

Serve over steamed rice.

Nutrition: Calories: 445Fat: 12 g Saturated fat: 4g Carbohydrates: 67 g Sugar: 1 g Fibers: 9 g Protein: 17 g Sodium: 670 mg

78. Rattlesnake Pasta from Pizzeria Uno

Preparation Time: 5 minutes

Cooking Time: 25 minutes

Servings: 6

Ingredients:

4 quarts - 1-pound penne pasta - 1 dash of salt

Chicken:

2 tablespoons butter - 2 cloves garlic, finely chopped

½ tablespoon Italian seasoning

1-pound chicken breast, boneless and skinless, cut into small squares

Sauce:

4 tablespoons butter - 2 cloves garlic, finely chopped

¼ cup all-purpose flour - 1 tablespoon salt

¾ teaspoon white pepper - 2 cups milk

1 cup half-and-half

¾ cup Parmesan cheese, shredded

8 ounces Colby cheese, shredded

3 jalapeno peppers, chopped

Directions:

In a pot of boiling water, add salt, and cook pasta according to package directions. Drain well and set aside.

To prepare the chicken, heat butter in a pan. Sauté garlic and Italian seasoning for 1 minute. Include chicken and cook 5-7 minutes or until cooked altogether, flipping midway through. Transfer onto a plate once. Set aside. In the same pan, prepare the sauce. Add butter and heat until melted. Blend in garlic and cook for 30 seconds. Then, add flour, salt, and pepper. Cook for 2 more minutes, stirring continuously. Pour in milk and half-and-half. Keep stirring until sauce turns thick and smooth.

Toss in chicken, jalapeno peppers, and pasta. Stir until combined.

Serve.

Nutrition: Calories: 835 Fat: 44 g Carbohydrates: 72 g Protein: 40 g Sodium: 1791 mg

79. Kung Pao Spaghetti from California Pizza Kitchen

Preparation Time: 10 minutes

Cooking Time: 20 minutes

Servings: 4

Ingredients:

1-pound spaghetti

2 tablespoons vegetable oil

3 chicken breasts, boneless and skinless

Salt and pepper, to taste

4 garlic cloves, finely chopped

½ cup dry roasted peanuts

6 green onions, cut into half-inch pieces

10-12 dried bird eyes hot peppers

Sauce:

½ cup soy sauce

½ cup chicken broth

½ cup dry sherry

2 tablespoons red chili paste with garlic

¼ cup sugar

2 tablespoons red wine vinegar

2 tablespoons cornstarch

1 tablespoon sesame oil

Directions:

Follow directions on package to cook spaghetti noodles. Drain and set aside.

Add oil to a large pan over medium-high heat. Liberally season chicken with salt and pepper, at that point include to dish once hot. Cook for about 3 to 4 minutes. Turn chicken over and cook for another 3 to 4 minutes. Remove from heat and allow to cool.

Blend together all sauce in a bowl.

Once chicken is cool sufficient to handle, chop chicken into little pieces. Set aside.

Return pan to heat. Add garlic and sauté for about 1 minute until aromatic. Pour in prepared sauce, then stir. Once bubbling, lower warm and permit to stew for almost 1 to 2 minutes or until fluid thickens. Add pasta,

cooked chicken, peanuts, hot peppers, and scallions.
Mix well.

Serve.

Nutrition: Calories: 548 Fat: 22 g Saturated fat: 7g
Carbohydrates: 67 g Sugar: 16 g Fibers: 4 g Protein:
15 g Sodium: 2028 mg

80. Three Cheese Chicken Penne from Applebee's

Preparation Time: 10 minutes

Cooking Time: 1 hour

Servings: 4

Ingredients:

2 boneless skinless chicken breasts

1 cup Italian salad dressing

3 cups penne pasta

6 tablespoons olive oil, divided

15 ounces Alfredo sauce

8 ounces combination mozzarella, Parmesan, and provolone cheeses, grated

4 roma tomatoes, seeded and diced

4 tablespoons fresh basil, diced

2 cloves garlic, finely chopped

Shredded parmesan cheese for serving

Directions:

Preheat oven to 350°F. In a bowl, add chicken then drizzle with Italian dressing. Mix to coat chicken with dressing fully. Cover using plastic wrap and keep inside refrigerator overnight but, if you're in a hurry, at least 2 hours is fine. Follow directions on package to cook penne pasta. Drain, then set aside. Brush 3 tablespoons oil onto grates of grill then preheat to medium-high heat. Add marinated chicken onto grill, discarding the marinade. Cook chicken until both sides are fully cooked and internal temperature measures 165°F. Remove from grill. Set aside until cool enough to handle. Then, cut chicken into thin slices. In a large bowl, add cooked noodles, Alfredo sauce, and grilled chicken. Mix until combined. Drizzle remaining oil onto large casserole pan, then pour noodle mixture inside. Sprinkle cheeses on top. Bake for about 15-20 minutes or until cheese turns a golden and edges of mixture begins to bubble. Remove from oven. Mix tomatoes, basil, and garlic in a bowl. Add on top of pasta. Sprinkle parmesan cheese before serving.

Nutrition: Calories: 1402 Fat: 93g Saturated fat: 27g Carbohydrates: 91g Sugar: 7g Fibers: 3g Protein: 62g Sodium: 5706mg

81. Red Lobster's Garlic Shrimp Scampi

Preparation Time: 15 minutes

Cooking Time: 15 minutes

Servings: 4

Ingredients

1-pound shrimp, peeled and deveined

Salt and pepper to taste - 1 tablespoon olive oil

3 garlic cloves, finely chopped - 1½ white wine

2 tablespoons lemon juice - ¼ teaspoon dried basil

¼ teaspoon dried oregano

¼ teaspoon dried rosemary

¼ teaspoon dried thyme

½ cup butter

2 tablespoons parsley leaves, minced

¼ cup Parmesan cheese, shredded (optional)

Directions

Flavor shrimp with salt and pepper.

In a pan with heated oil, sauté shrimp on medium-high heat for about 2 minutes or until color changes to pink. Transfer onto a plate for later.

In the same pan, sauté garlic for 30 seconds or until aromatic. Pour in white wine and lemon juice. Stir, then bring to a boil. Adjust heat to medium-low and cook for an additional 4 minutes. Mix in basil, oregano, rosemary, and thyme. Then, add butter gradually. Mix until completely melted and blended with other ingredients. Remove from heat.

Return shrimp to pan and add parsley. Taste and adjust seasoning with salt and pepper as needed.

Sprinkle Parmesan on top, if desired. Serve.

Nutrition: Calories 448, Total Fat 29 g, Carbohydrates 3 g, Protein 26 g, Sodium 362 mg

82. DIY Red Hook's Lobster Pound

Preparation Time: 10 minutes

Cooking Time: 10 minutes

Servings: 2

Ingredients

2 large egg yolks

1 teaspoon Dijon mustard

4 teaspoons fresh lemon juice, plus more

1 cup vegetable oil

Coarse salt and ground pepper, to taste

¾ pounds lobster meat, cooked and chopped into 1-inch cubes

2 top-split hot dog rolls

2 tablespoons butter, melted

Iceberg lettuce, shredded

1 scallion, finely sliced

Paprika, to taste

Directions

To make the DIY mayonnaise, add egg yolks, mustard, and lemon juice to a food processor. Process until fully mixed. Then, while still processing, gradually add oil until mixture thickens and becomes cloudy. Add salt and pepper.

Transfer to a bowl and cover. Set aside.

Prepare lobster filling by combining lobster pieces, prepared mayonnaise, lemon juice, salt, and pepper in a bowl.

Heat griddle. Apply butter to insides of hotdog rolls. Place rolls to grill butter side down and cook until golden brown.

Assemble lobster rolls by layering lettuce, lobster and mayonnaise mixture, scallions, and paprika. Repeat for 2nd lobster roll.

Serve.

Nutrition: Calories 1746, Total fat 135 g, Saturated fat 90 g, Carbohydrates 49 g, Sugar 9 g, Fibers 5 g, Protein 92 g, Sodium 2299 mg

Conclusion

If you are a food-driven soul, having a really good meal is one of the great pleasures of life. Such a reward may be even the administrative labor of dining out— making a reservation, getting ready and, of course, settling down to order. But the most magical moment of all is when the long-awaited food arrives– gliding through a crowed dining room and ready to be enjoyed before being put on the table. Including beautifully designed salads and incredibly well crispy, delicious fried all things to silky spaghetti and perfectly cooked steaks— good food for the restaurants always seems to have a little extra to make it show.

But if you've ever badly prepared food of this kind on your own, there is hope! With fair a couple of straightforward traps and tips, you can also cook quality cuisine in your own kitchen. These are tricks that may not seem so strong on their own but can transform how you prepare and produce food when they are all used together. These tips help you cook at home like a pro from expired spices and how you use salt to arrange it before you start cooking literally.

Dishes in restaurants are often rich in oil, spices and salt, whereas packaged foods are usually full of sodium and supplements. However, home-made foods are usually more nutritious and contain fewer calories. Because when you cook yourself, you control what ingredients you use and how much they contain, explains Nutritionist Sarah Jacobs, one of the founders of the NYC Wellness Project, a consulting firm that works with companies to improve employee health. In addition, you tend to serve restaurant-size portions that are often large enough to feed two or three people, or to get dessert or cocktails. When we cook at home, we do it differently, which reduces the possibility of adding unnecessary things in moderation. A healthy regular diet, homemade food can even improve the way you eat between meals. Once you're usual to eating solid and nutritious food at domestic, you'll discover merely are looking somewhere else. For example, children are better off eating fruit or carrots in a playground or at a party, even if they are offered fast food, no matter how tempting.

Spending time with family and friends is important for the good of all. It can prevent loneliness associated with depression, heart disease and dangerous illnesses. With a little effort, cooking can help you become more social. Have your children go to the kitchen with you - give them simple tasks when they are young - or cook with friends. In case you need to create modern companions, consider cooking classes where you can interact with classmates as you learn new skills. And do not reduce social benefits that you get when your meal is ready. Many women are happy to be able to offer homemade food to friends and family at various events. Food is usually met with a smiling face and a desire to return.

Either in groups or alone, cooking doesn't just fill your stomach. It can also improve your mental and physical health - benefits that you will enjoy long after eating. Improving your culinary skills (or developing new ones) can improve your diet and social life. We tend to cook less as we get older. Why cook when you can cover something in microwave, pour something that is ready in a bowl, or use a speed dial to remove it? But this fast food trend has pushed many men to choose a diet that puts them at risk of gaining weight, heart disease, and diabetes. Dr. David Eisenberg from the Harvard T.H. Nutrition Department the Chan School of Public Health says that many older men never develop or lose their skills in the kitchen and therefore become dependent on processed and processed foods. But cooking is easier than you think.

As you improve your skill and you feel more comfortable while you cook, you might find that your culinary interests extend beyond the kitchen. Doctor Eisenberg said that you get to know different foods such as locally grown vegetables, meat, fruits and herbs better, become more experienced food sellers and know what to look for. In addition, you might find that increasing your cooking skills can also warm your social life. You'll be able build a closer relationship along with your accomplice since you're both more involved in nourishment planning and may be propelled to welcome others to share dishes you have got arranged. In expansion, cooking can be an unwinding and unwinding action that you just can appreciate yourself. Individuals discover individual fulfillment in cooking for themselves or see experience as a way to engage with their creativity. Cooking is no longer a boring thing, but something that gives them great pleasure.

Cooking is fun, it is a passion to share with friends and with those you love. Cooking is a gesture to be safeguarded which, unfortunately, today risks being set aside for the chaotic and hectic life we lead and, therefore, for the needs related to the short time. Today, for a healthy and pleasant family meal, we prefer "fast food", ready meals or a paltry "packed lunch". All of this, not a fault, is a necessity today

Lightning Source UK Ltd.
Milton Keynes UK
UKHW021127191120
373690UK00011B/886